CELEBRATING LIFE

CELEBRATING LIFE

RITES OF PASSAGE FOR ALL AGES

TZIPORA KLEIN

Delphi Press, Inc. ■ *Oak Park, Illinois*

Published 1992 by Delphi Press, Inc., Oak Park, Illinois, 60304. All rights reserved. No part of this book may be reproduced in any form, in print or electronically, except for brief excerpts used in newspaper or magazine reviews, without the written consent of the publisher.

97 96 95 94 93 92 5 6 4 3 2 1

ISBN 0-878980-05-X

Library of Congress Catalogue Card Number 92-070475

The paper used in this publication meets the minimum requirements of American National Standard for Information Services—Permanence of Paper for Printed Library Materials, ANSIZ39 48-1984.

The text of this book is printed on recycled paper

CONTENTS

For my parents who gave me the gift of life and laughter.

For my Craft parents who gave me the Moon and Sun.

And for my family who taught me why it was important.

ACKNOWLEDGMENTS

My first thanks must go to my best friend and husband Kenny. His support and "pre-editing" made this a much less frightening undertaking. Next, my two children, Maeghan and Jesse for loaning me to the computer long enough to get the manuscript finished.

Thanks also to Kurt for the loan of the computer itself and to George for teaching me about technology. A note to Sean Hunt for helping me overcome my basic fear of computers.

And thanks to my editor, and now friend, Karen Jackson for all her wise words about trees to keep me inspired.

There have been many people across the United States that have helped by making the coffee and keeping me fed both physically and spiritually. None have been more inspiring or full of caffeine as Cecil, thanks.

A special thank-you to Tammara James, my Craft sister and long time friend, for sharing ritual ideas with me over the last fifteen years. The same to Michele Dileo for her willingness to share what she knows. Much the same for Brad, my personal metaphysician.

Lastly, thanks to my own Blue Star family, for putting up with me and being the test group for so many of the rituals in this book.

"Words should never be taken as an absolute. Here then are the words as they exist for the moment. With the blessings of the God and Goddess, they will change and remain the same."

—Blue Star Book of Shadows

INTRODUCTION

You have come upon this doorway in search of magick.
Why do you ask to be shown something you have always
known in your own heart? You stand now on the threshold
of your own dreams. If you can find the courage to enter,
new worlds will open before you. The very trees that you
have sat beneath, will seem to shift in their dance, and
sway to a music so sweet that it can break your heart. Will
you find the courage to enter and forever change your
world?

— from a traditional ritual

Our lives are a series of experiences. Each experience offers
us an opportunity to grow and to learn new things about
ourselves and our interactions with the world around us. Yet,
people often ignore the beauty and possibility of the moment
and reach for things far ahead or beyond. As they devote
energy to a distant event, they ignore the joy that fill everyday
events. "Life" is mundane existence. They forget how to
truly live.

Each experience, each everyday moment is important. To
celebrate the everyday joys and to reconcile yourself to sorrow
and disappointment is to understand the difference between
existing and living life to its fullest.

I believe that each day is a magickal act. If you look at life
from this perspective, you too will find a way to view every
experience in a new and more meaningful way. The little

accomplishments are just as important as the major mile-stones.

I wrote this book to help you to learn to identify moments of change and share with you the joy I have found by enacting a ritual to mark their significance. I hope that after reading this book you will create rituals to celebrate your own rites of passage.

We have all heard the term "rites of passage" before, but may not have thought of applying that term to our own experiences. Our western society depicts a rite of passage as a dramatic experience through which maturity is gained and innocence lost. This way of thinking denies the personal and spiritual changes all people experience as they live and grow, age and die. It is crucial to our personal growth and evolution to reclaim rites of passage as a right and benefit of living our lives to the fullest. From a simple blessing done alone to a large and formal ritual, a rite of passage enables us to integrate the art of noticing into each day's experience. That which has been denied or declared unimportant by the greater society *is* important. We must bless ourselves and our lives in order to change and to heal ourselves, to raise our children well, and ultimately to save our fragile living planet.

ABOUT THIS BOOK AND HOW TO USE IT

Before you do anything else, read all of this introduction. This will introduce you to the terms used in every ritual and enable you to use any ritual or read any chapter independent of the others. This is important, because you may want to start this book somewhere in the middle. It is also important that you know before you start what this book *isn't*.

Again, I cannot emphasize this enough, *all moments of your individual experience may be perceived as moments of growth and initiation. Any moment you choose may be marked with a rite of passage.* It is up to *you* to notice them and assess their value. magick is created by a subtle shift in perception. Magick is not created by following a set of directions, just as the value of your life may not be assessed by other's expectations. Magick begins by recognizing that which is unique and important to you and grasping it and holding it close to your heart.

This book is a collection of maps, outlines and stories of wisdom gained from my experiences. In these pages I share with you things I was lucky enough to experience or that I was shown along my path. Many rituals are presented in script form. I offer them as guidelines. This book is not a collection of great and esoteric teachings carved in stone and never to be altered.

Indeed, I hope that you change all my words and adapt them to your personal circumstances. A rite of passage is not something that occurs the same way every time in every life, suspended in time and cut away from the world. A rite of passage is a growing and vital experience that should be lived and absorbed into your being to strengthen and nourish you.

Not all of the rituals presented here will be suitable to your needs or desires. During the early stages of writing the book, a dear friend commented that I had not included a ritual for a baby's first haircut. I thanked her for her suggestion, but quickly pointed out that I also did not include a ritual for the first bath or the first illness although these are also passages in life worthy of ritual. Like my friend you may find that something you think is significant is left out or that something trivial is touted as important. You will soon be able to recognize these moments and create the rites to mark them for yourself.

The book is organized by groups of experiences. It need not be read in the order presented. For instance, I've chosen to start this book with a ritual to celebrate conception. You may not nave considered having children yet or perhaps will not have children or have children who are grown. You may have no use for rituals that celebrate birth and child-rearing. You may have picked up this book during a time of grieving or illness. Use this book according to your needs.

The first few chapters center on conception, childbirth and early childhood. The middle chapters are about moving into and through adulthood. Here you will find rituals ranging from celebrating your first sexual union through becoming grandparents. There rituals for new homes, jobs and celebrating betrothal and marriage.

The final chapter of the book recognizes that not all of life is a celebration. Many important and significant events in our lives are accompanied by tears of sorrow. Although there are so many different kinds of losses, far more than would seem to fit in a single chapter, the grieving process is very similar in each circumstance. Therefore I have devoted one chapter specifically to grief.

While grief is greatly eased by sharing, I offer a few cautions about approaching the grief of others. At a moment of sorrow, whether the grief of a young person who has just experienced the break-up of their first romance or the grief experienced by someone who has lost a life's partner, a person has little perspective about the loss. When tears of sorrow flow, they flow with the same intensity no matter what the reason. As we grow in experience and wisdom, we develop a more mature perspective. Never give advice or orders about how to pull together and never tell them how it could be worse. Our purpose here is not to try to determine which kind of loss is more important but rather to acknowledge and ease the pain.

The void that is created by loss, no matter the type of loss, can be viewed as a place to be filled with new understanding. As we grow and recover from loss, perspective towards the loss will grow and eventually change. A rite of passage revolving around grief and loss seeks to assist a move away from this void and towards this stronger, altered viewpoint. Tears of sorrow must be encouraged to evolve, however slowly, towards comfort and empowerment.

A CIRCLE OF FAMILY AND FRIENDS

Throughout this book I constantly refer to those people whom you may want to include in your rituals. I call this group your Circle. I have modeled these rituals after the traditional Circles from my particular practice of Wicca, but it may not be appropriate for you. There are no hard and fast rules that dictate who should be included in your Circle. If you and your family are already involved with a working ritual group, then you will likely be inviting them to work with you in celebrating rites of passage. People who share a common spiritual path will naturally comprise the majority of your Circle.

In some ways, inviting friends or family members to your rituals is very similar to going to a church to celebrate a traditional milestone event—a christening or a wedding. But some rituals presented here will be unlike anything they ever saw in a church. You probably have special friends or family members who do not share your particular outlet. If you wish to invite these people to take part in your rituals, by all means do so. But I suggest you do them the great courtesy of explaining what will be happening beforehand so that they will be at ease with your intentions, language and symbolism. Be understanding and do not be disappointed if they choose not to participate.

When people come together to celebrate or witness these rituals, a deep bonding takes place. This bonding can release significant and powerful emotions. Know this, and exercise careful judgement when you ask your friends and family to take active roles in the rituals. These rituals are based on archetypical forms and relate to deity in a very primal way. They often take participants completely by surprise and open up part of their psyches that may otherwise go unnoticed or repressed. Emotions run high at these times and seem to override "normal" thinking. To avoid any possible difficulty, I further suggest that those with the most active roles meet several times beforehand to discuss the ritual and make any necessary adjustments to fit specific needs beforehand.

Remember that not every rite of passage will require a full Circle or elaborate choreography. Often these rituals will simply occur as part of a normal day. When that is the case you should celebrate freely and take special note of how magick has entered your life. The goal is to mark these events, these accomplishments, and these transformations. The means, tools and people included are secondary.

WHAT MAKES THE RITUAL?

Since many of the rituals presented in this book are scripted, it is important to be acquainted with the formats used. Again, I use approaches derived from traditional Wicca, but these are only one of many possible ways. After becoming comfortable with the flow of the rituals, you may well decide to change the order of things or leave out those parts that are not comfortable for your family. It would be impossible to write this book without reflecting my own feelings towards deity and ritual. The words I may choose, the names, the order are not what is really important. The celebration of change and growth within family is what is to be emphasized, not semantics.

Ritual Baths

Many people enjoy taking the time before entering a ritual space to have a bath. This is not a "washing" bath, where you use soap and shampoo to wash away the grime of everyday living. A ritual bath is a place where, sitting in warm, usually scented water, you can cleanse your spirit. Some may choose to take a private bath at home before arriving for the ritual itself. Many people enjoy the group bonding of preparing a common bath where each person will symbolically bathe by merely wetting a part of their body. Still others will choose to share a common bath with Circle family and friends. It is a moment to return to the womb of the Mother, and release anxiety and tensions. This is a safe place to center yourselves and prepare for the ritual you are about to enter. It is common practice to place some sea salt in the bath, for its cleansing and relaxing properties as well as herbs and oils that are compatible with the theme of the ritual itself. (See Appendix IV for ritual bath ideas and suggestions.)

Sweeping

Before participants enter the ritual space, the youngest dedicated female present takes a broom and "sweeps" away all unwanted thoughts and influences. She is the Maiden aspect, of the Goddess: strong of will and filled with all of life's promise. The broom moving about the Circle deosil (clockwise) reminds us of the never ending and always changing cycles of life around us.

Mixing Salt and Water

Water represents our emotions, so we begin by casting aside those feelings that are unwanted in our sacred space. We ask for confusion, malice, insecurity, loneliness to leave us. In their place we ask for tranquility, compassion, love and wholeness. The salt is the symbol of nature's law. It is also there to remind us that promises made are not empty words. We ask for the special blessings of strength, honor and wisdom. By placing salt in the Water we are demonstrating a balance between both our emotions and rational thinking. Only through this union will our lives be balanced and fulfilling.

Casting the Circle

Here is where we truly begin to create sacred space. Casting the Circle defines an area that will act as a focal point for what we are doing. The Circle contains energy and helps the participants to focus it. It may be cast by physically walking in a circle to describe the space or by verbally invoking it. In ancient British mythology and lore the wand was always used to cast the enchantments. Wands and bells summoned the wee folk, the fairy folk. These woke the spirits of the land and brought the attention of the Goddess and God. So, with wand in hand we proclaim that for this time, while we are gathered here, this is a place that is sacred and apart from the everyday world.

Blessing with the Elements

Our space is defined and stands ready. Like a beautiful crystal bowl, our Circle can be filled now with those things we wish to bring to us. What better way than to fill this space with the four elements? We call upon each in turn to join us and bring us all closer to all that the element symbolizes. These are the building blocks of life: Air, Fire, Water and Earth. All life is made up of these four, and to give life to the Circle we bless not just the space, but the participants with all four elements. The elements may be represented in the Circle by incense, or perhaps a pretty fan, for Air; by a candle for Fire; a cup of Water, and a living plant or a crystal or rock or dish of salt for Earth. By taking a moment to acknowledge the elements with all of our senses, we also further our awareness of Their presence in everyday life. Each ritual will build on those before it, and so each time we call for these blessings we return in part to the very first time Their influence was called upon by our ancestors. Knowing this our elemental blessing is a moment of frozen time, returning us all to our ancient roots.

Censing and Asperging

We can ask for the blessings of the four elements in another fashion. By combining Air and Fire in incense we can cense the Circle. The act of carrying about incense in this way is similar to the Native Peoples ritual of smudging. Using the sweet Air, we cleanse away negative thoughts and inhale the breath of the Gods. In asperging, or sprinkling, we combine salt (Earth) and Water and bring the balance of the two. Washing away sadness, only joy can remain.

Some may choose to do both, others will decide on one or the other. Whether you bless your Circle with each element separately, or in combination, keep in mind the reason you ask for these blessings. By listening to your own inner voice, you will find that whichever you do will be right for the moment.

Calling the Quarters

With the building of the Circle complete we can invite the Spirits of the Directions to join us. We ask them to come to be with us and share in our ritual, not to do our will or protect us. Since we believe that we are all interconnected with each other and all that is divine, there is nothing to fear here. In calling the quarters we ask an honored friend and guest to be present. We greet these spirits with respect and ask that each give us a special gift that is unique to them. In this way all share in these gifts and they are intensified by that sharing.

Calling the God and Goddess

Ancient people saw the divine expressed in all life around them. It was believed that there were names for these divine beings. These are the Gods and Goddesses of which I speak. Whether you call upon the name of the ancient Egyptian Mother or the Navaho Sky Father, the Gods that hear you and answer have lived on this Earth since before time. In today's world we are often cut off from this spark of all creation, and through the ages of history the names and methods of calling upon that very spark has been changed and transformed. Many in our culture see the cross as the symbol of the divine. Before that others may have used a star. And earlier still a circle. But no matter what the symbol, there was never a time before the Gods themselves.

We call Them into our Circle now to bring that spark to all gathered. We see the reflection of the God and Goddess in all around us now, and are once again reconnected to our roots.

Statement of Intent

Our Circle is now complete. We have asked for the Goddess, God and the Four Directions to join us. A moment is needed to regather our energies and focus our attention on the purpose for the ritual. A simple statement of intent will do this in very short order. By taking this moment to center on the purpose of the ritual we also allow participants an opportunity to ground themselves and prepare for the body of the rite. This is especially important for people who get carried off by the shifting energies around them during the casting.

The Ritual

Now we get to the reason we gathered together. The body of each ritual will vary in both format and style. Since each ritual reflects a different passage in life, it follows that each ritual will take on a slightly different form and tone. What does remain constant for all rituals is the attitude held by the participants. There should be a feeling of reverence, but not so severe that people feel afraid to laugh where appropriate or move about if that feels correct. Remember that the Gods we have asked to be a part of these rites have created not only the Sunset but also the duck-billed platypus. They too have a sense of humor.

The Sharing

In families or ritual groups such as the one that I was fortunate enough to learn the Craft from, after the formal part of the ritual is over the important part begins. For us, this was in the form of a sharing. All in the Circle are encouraged to tell a story or sing a song that relates to the ritual. Many great words of wisdom are passed on in this way. There is also feeling of being part of the family when all share a part of themselves. When young children are part of the ritual, you might consider adding a short game of some sort at this point.

Wine and Cakes

Singing and storytelling make for a relaxed atmosphere. They also can lead to thirsty people and building appetites. Wine and Cakes is a way to share food and drink with each other and to take time to say "thank you" to the Earth that gave us all the bounty. The wine may in fact be a fruit juice or milk. There is no reason why anyone should feel the need to consume alcohol if they are not comfortable with it. When wine is offered, it is only a taste that we share. The cakes may be in the form of crackers, sweet breads, or fruit pieces. We share something seasonal to connect with the Mother. We also give back a small bit of the food and drink by pouring out a libation into a bowl; later this will be left on the ground for the Mother to take back.

The ritual has filled us spiritually. The sharing has warmed our hearts. By sharing the food and drink in Circle we nurture each other. Old customs in the British Isles held that once you shared food and drink (in some towns bread and salt) you were bound to never speak ill of one another. Many customs such as this were based in wisdom and caring. Not only did this custom strengthen the feelings within the extended family, but it reinforced the sacred attitudes towards all meals shared outside of the ritual space as well. In ways such as this we begin to see the connection of Circle life to mundane or everyday life.

Closing the Circle

Now that the Wine and Cakes have been finished and all work of the ritual concluded, it is time to close the ritual itself. As we prepare to leave the ritual space, we take time to say thank you and good-bye, acknowledging for the last time in the ritual the presence of the divine. By thanking and parting with the Goddesses and Gods and then the Quarters we re-enter the mundane world. This states in a magickal sense that we are finished. In ritual, as in all things, we have a human need to make note of a conclusion. In this way we also give ourselves a chance to shift gears and prepare to get on with everyday life again.

The Feast

Ritual has ended, but the after-glow of the Circle is still in the Air. In order to enjoy that feeling, to continue the sense of family sharing or support, we have a feast. This does not have to be a catered affair. Many of my most memorable feasts were pot luck with everyone bringing a dish to share. We gather in a different room, or little way from the ritual area to eat. Stories are shared, friendly gossip begins and we are joined as friends. In many ways, the casual atmosphere that we are in now allows the magick to take hold. We share a very special part of ourselves in ritual space, but to stay together for awhile afterwards makes a strong statement of commitment to each other. During the feasting we can move and speak freely, without the formality of the ritual. Now we can offer feedback to one another and share a different dimension of our spiritual lives.

The Altar and Tools

"Preparing the altar" sounds so formal. Our altars are any surface, be they a beautiful table, or finished tree stump or simply the floor of our living room or the forest floor. The altar is merely the physical space upon which we set the tools or ritual props we need. You may wish to make a small ritual of preparing the area by perhaps washing the top of a table or setting out a beautiful cloth. The more conscious thought you put into the preparations, the more they will lead to a deeper significance for you. Many rituals do not have any specific need for an altar, while others need one only to lend a sense of order to the tools or other symbols you might desire to use. However you decide on the surface, remember that it is your attitude and approach that makes the altar special.

Tools are ritual props. You may have a special cup that is used only for rituals. A wand is traditionally made out of wood, not metal. The lovely thing about many traditions is their flexibility, so while many will choose to use only wood, others may set a precedent in their rituals to use metal or wood wound with copper and stones. The notion of wood in part comes from the British Isles where the wand (wood) cast the enchantment and the knife (iron) broke it. Some may not use a wand at all.

Ritual knives are also something that is relatively new to a religion of the common people. It is not likely that our ancestors had beautiful knives set aside, but rather used what was handy when cutting was needed for a specific purpose. Today however, many people enjoy the beauty of a well-made blade and use one with pride. I have met some people who used a crystal with a well defined terminated point in lieu of a blade. If this works for you, then there is very little likelihood of the world falling apart because you have chosen to use a different tool. Use only those tools which make you feel good about what you are doing.

The incense that is used in ritual is another important tool. You may choose to use stick or cone incense that can be purchased from many places such as New Age bookstores and Oriental gift shops. Or perhaps you are creative and wish to mix your own herbs and oils to have an incense that is unique for your ritual. By blending various herbs and oils based on their planetary or emotional qualities, you can then experiment and create a different incense for every purpose. (See Appendices II and IV for some formula ideas.) I have provided simple recipes throughout the book. When mixing herbs in these recipes, note that a "part" is simply an equal measure, such as a teaspoon or a palmfull of an herb. If you decide to blend your own incense you will need to purchase a roll of self-igniting charcoal. This charcoal is specially made for burning incense. This charcoal will burn extremely hot so place it in a dish with sand, salt or kitty litter in the bottom to absorb the heat. The incense is placed on top of the coal where it will quickly begin to burn.

Since candles are used in so many of the rituals, you may wish to set aside a few candle holders that you use only for rituals. They can be made of anything that safely holds the candles. Silver, copper, wood and glass all have a very definite feel to them. Experiment with many types or try making your own.

Bells were rung to waken the spirits of the land, so you might wish to add a bell or small gong to your collection of ritual tools. The same goes for drums and other small instruments. Learn to hear what your own inner voice is telling you about your choices and follow that voice.

Your tools will change over time. This will be because as you work more and more with them your perspectives will shift, or your own attitudes change. Another likely reason for this is because people give each other gifts. What nicer way to say thank you to someone than to use that new cup in an upcoming ritual?

A final word about tools and your children. If you are including your children in rituals, then you might want to consider letting them have a few special tools of their own. This will underscore what it is you are sharing and help to make them feel more a part of what is happening in the Circle. Do use common sense when considering what is safe in their hands. Even something as simple as a candle snuffer can present a problem if not supervised. And don't be surprised if you walk in on your little ones playing ritual games if they get their hands on the tools, it is one of the more wonderful benefits of shared rituals.

Priest and Priestess

A few of the rituals require roles of Priest and Priestess. A Priest and Priestess may be anyone of your choosing. You may ask the most experiences ritualists to play these roles, special friends, or simply assign them to members of your regular Circle. Priest and Priestess facilitate the ritual. They do not need to be people of special status or training.

There are many good books filled with ideas and examples of ritual technique. If you are interested in learning more, I recommend *Spiral Dance* by Starhawk; *The Art of Ritual* by Renee Beck and Sydney Barbara Metrick; and *The Witches Way* by Janet and Stuart Farrar. Ultimately, your own creativity and imagination will come forth and your ritual will reflect your own taste and personality.

If viewed through magickal eyes, each day may become a Rite of Passage. May each of you reading these pages be blessed with the gift of those eyes and may your hearts filled with music and laughter.

1

LIFE'S BEGINNING

I am the beginning of all life. From the great whale to the
tiny infant, I have taught the mysteries of the ages to all who
would ask, and have been as a midwife at every birth. It was I
who first guided your steps, and I rejoiced with each new
wonder explored. Though you have called me by many
names, in many places, I was first your Mother.

—from a traditional blessing

Mother. Father. Home and hearth. These are the very first
things we experience in our lives. As newborns we look to our
parents as reflections of the God and Goddess themselves,
without whom we would surely never survive. Toddlers see
parents as magickal beings capable of doing wondrous feats,
such as reaching top shelves and making food and comfort
appear as needed. What child has not sought comfort in the
arms and laps of his/her parents when nighttime monsters
awoke them?

These earliest years are the foundation of our relationships
for the rest of our lifetime. We now know that children who
are well nurtured and loved grow into caring adults filled with
security and responsibility. Those children who are unfortunate and are not given these very basic needs all too often
grow into suspicious people, with streaks of self-hatred. By
fostering an attitude filled with wonder of the world around
us, and celebrating all phases of life, we give ourselves and our
children many more opportunities to share warmth and
caring.

As adults we can sometimes forget the small victories in a child's life. Without thinking, we fix ourselves food, or with long-skilled hands maneuver about our daily tasks. Our children must learn each one of these. By celebrating these accomplishments with rites of passage we acknowledge their importance to our children, and recapture that sense of wonder for ourselves.

There really are no hard and fast rules about what deserves a ritual and what does not. Yet there is need for a word of caution here. If we begin to ritualize everything in a formal way, or work hard to "do it by the book," we risk losing the magick of the moment. Always remember that it may be far better for our children to have a short rite and many hours of shared time with family and friends, than to have to listen to endless lines of ritual litany. For those who have resisted the idea of adding spirituality to the lives of their children, I believe that it is their memories of hours upon hours of being forced to sit still that has left them with such a bitter taste toward ritual. This is a path upon which we learn to see all magick in the world around us, not of strict rules and stuffy liturgy.

CONCEPTION

The first celebration of life centers on a child newly conceived. It is comfortable to write this ritual for a male-female couple. However, thought and imagination should go into the preparation of any ritual, and the rituals in this book may be adapted to the circumstances of any group or family.

Life begins in Water, as it has always begun. So this ritual is set in a bathtub, stream, lake, or any body of Water. If you are using a bathtub for the ritual, you may want to add some sea salt and flower petals to the Water. If you are outside, you can scatter flower petals on the Water.

Gifts from friends and family should be brought and set out near the tub, or if the ritual is to move into a common space, in the common area. Food and drink should be prepared ahead of time. If you are lucky enough to have a space outside, set up the gifts and altar beside the Water.

You will need herbal washes and incense.

Female herbal wash
2 parts life everlasting
2 parts motherwort
1 part rose petals
1/2 part woodruff
a few drops of lotus oil

Male herbal wash
1 part patchouli
1 part vetivert
1 part vervain
1/2 part sandalwood
1/2 part oak

To make the washes, fill separate pitchers with 2 to 3 quarts of boiling Water. Steep the herbs in the Water for about 30 minutes. Let cool and strain.

Incense
2 parts sandalwood
1 part rosebuds
1 part cedar
1 part lavender
a few drops of honey

Blend well and burn over charcoal.

It is appropriate to burn candles during any ritual. For this one, yellow is suggested, for it is a color that is associated with new beginnings.

RITUAL TO CELEBRATE CONCEPTION

Casting the Circle

Both parents enter the Water together, face each other, and hold hands.

Woman: The Circle is cast around us.
     As it is in the Mother's womb.

Man: A Circle is formed in love
     As the Mother conceives all lives in love.

Together: Our Circle is formed
     In nurturing and love.
     Blessed be.

Man: I call on the Spirits of East
     Creatures of Air, playful Sylphs,
     Join us and renew our minds.

Woman: I call on the Spirits of South.
     Creatures of Fire, dancing Salamanders,
     Be here and sustain our passion.

Man: I call on the Spirits of West.
     Creatures of Water, gentle Undines.
     Join us and embrace us with love.

Woman: I call on the Spirits of North.

Creatures of Earth, wise Gnomes.
Be here and deepen our commitment to each
other.

Together: We welcome the Four Directions and the gifts
that each brings here. We thank Them for
Their presence.

Woman: I ask that the Mother of All be with us here.
She who has given birth to all creatures, and
has nurtured all of Her children. Great
Mother come to us in Your many names, and
share in our joy.

Man: I ask that the Father of All be with us here.
He who has given of His seed, and taught
great mysteries to all who would learn them.
Gentle Father, come to us in Your many
names, and be part of our happiness.

Blessings

Woman: *(Takes pitcher of male herbal wash and slowly*   unfortunate
pours it over partner.) Life cannot exist with   typos
the seed. Through our love, you have given
me your seed to bring new life to this world, a
life that we will work together to love and
nurture. Tonight is yours, a night to honor
you for this gift. You sit as my friend and
lover, just as the Father of all life sits beside
the Mother.

Life comes from the Gods. From the Gods it
comes to the seed of man. From the seed of

man it flows to the womb of woman. Seed bearer, I love and honor you. Share this gift of life with me.

Man: *(Takes pitcher of female herb wash and slowly pours if over partner.)* Life has always come from the Mother's womb. Through our love, your womb now holds a new life, a life that we will work together to love and nurture. Tonight is yours, a night to honor you for this gift. You sit as my friend and lover, just as the Mother of all life sits beside the Father.

Life comes from the Gods. It is brought into this world through the Mother's womb. You are as the Mother of all things. Mother, I love you and honor you. Share this gift of new life with me.

The couple may now take a few moments to speak to the new child and share their feelings and hopes. They should end by saying:

Together: Blessed child, you will be welcomed to this world with love. Blessed be.

Here the couple may choose to sit in the bath for a few minutes and enjoy each other's company. When they are ready, they should dry each other off with large fluffy towels, and anoint each other with a light oil (such as sandalwood mixed with jasmine). If the conception is being celebrated by a Circle or larger family, the couple may then move into a common area or the Water's edge where children or other Circle members can join in the celebration. When the ritual is done in a bathtub, they may want to thank the Goddess and God and the four elements, and ask them to join the couple as they move into an area where the other members of the Circle have set up candles and other tools, and then cast a Circle around the room. The couple may invite children into the Circle.

Joining the Circle

If this child is to be the younger brother or sister to other children, the parents may now wish to provide a time during the ritual to let the other children speak to the baby in utero. This is a gentle way of allowing older children to feel that they, too, are important in the family, and that their feelings are being recognized. Often they will want to know whether this ritual was done for them when they were still in utero. The bonding that can occur by allowing the other children to take part in the ritual in this way cannot be over emphasized.

If there are feelings of jealousy, or fear, this might provide the older child(ren) with a moment to voice those feelings as well. It is not uncommon to hear a child say, "I hope that you're a boy so you don't mess with my dolls," or to inform the baby, "It's okay if you come to live with us, but I'm still boss around here." These feelings are normal and should be respected.

The partners, siblings, and other Circle members might exchange gifts after all have spoken. Food and drink should be shared, along with stories of the Goddess and God, especially in their aspects associated with lovemaking and fertility. Stories of Circle members' own conception and birth experiences are very appropriate.

Closing the Circle

If the couple left the bath area, and asked the Goddess, God, and Elemental Spirits to join them in the new Circle space, the closing can be adapted to include the entire family or group.

Woman: Mother Goddess, we thank you for Your presence. We ask that You bless our family, and always stay in our hearts.

Man: Father God, we thank You for being with us here. We ask that You guide and protect us, and always live in our hearts.

Together: May You return to Your homes in peace.

Man: Spirits of East, Creatures of Air. Thank you for joining us here. We send you home with a kiss. *(Kisses hand and offers to the direction.)* Blessed be.

Woman: Spirits of South, Creatures of Fire. Thank you for joining us here. We send you home with a kiss. Blessed be.

Man: Spirits West, Creatures of Water. Thank you for joining us here. We send you home with a kiss. Blessed be.

Woman: Spirits of North, Creatures of Earth. Thank you for joining us here. We send you home with a kiss. Blessed be.

Together: This Circle was formed in love, let it end in love. Blessed be.

Later, this ritual may be consecrated by the partners' making love to celebrate the conception of this life. They may light a yellow candle near the bed, and ask the Goddess and God to be present for this. If this has been a long-awaited pregnancy, additional celebration should include giving thanks for no longer needing to check calendars for optimum ovulation times. However you choose to do it, thanks should be given for the gift of life.

BIRTH

Welcoming a new person into this world is certainly a time of great celebration and change. If this is a first child, then the parents are going to adjust their lives in ways that they cannot possibly anticipate. In an established family, the arrival of a new child means the other family members must also make way for changes. Of course, the new baby is now facing a life outside of the womb, and needs to be made welcome.

There are several ways to approach this transition in a ritual form. How elaborate your ritual can be is often dependant on the environment into which the child is to be delivered. Many hospitals and alternative birthing centers will allow music or ritual props in the delivery room. If you are doing a home birth, then a full Circle casting may be easily incorporated into the birthing.

Other rituals may be performed at the time of the birth as well. For example, a group of close friends may get together to "connect" with the mother and to project for a smooth and easy labor and delivery. This was done during the birth of my daughter, who was born in a hospital, and that labor lasted for only three hours! Several members of my coven, and some non-coven friends, gathered in my home, or were in contact through a phone chain. The ritual in my home began with a bath of warm Water, to which baby oil and a few drops of sweet pea oil were added. The group then sat in a Circle and meditated, visualizing me remaining calm and in control. As an aid to meditation, they focused on the Empress card of the Tarot (for a key to this card, see Paul Foster Case's The Tarot). They visualized, seeing me pregnant and full, as well as content. The image then changed to that of the Crone, preparing for the separation. She was wise and experienced, kind yet stern. Since this was the end of the pregnancy, the Death card was used for the power of transformation. Through the Crone I would be able to let go of the pregnancy. Next they saw me holding my daughter (we knew it was a girl) and focused on the World card. Finally they used the Ten of Cups, to show a family content. Passing these Tarot images and thoughts around a Circle, a birth canal was formed by the group. At no time did anyone suggest that the labor move any faster than my body needed it to, nor did they try to intervene against the natural flow. Knowing that I had such a network of loving support helped me through the labor. Did it work? By the time the last person was contacted by way of the phone chain, we were calling from the hospital to announce the delivery!

If there has been a delay in the onset of labor, or some other complication, a ritual to ease the condition may be performed. When my son's due date was nearly two weeks past, my daughter (at the time she was about four) cast a Circle, had me light a red candle on her little altar, and asked for the "Fire Fairies" to help in her brother's birthing (she seemed to know the child's gender long before we did). She let the candle on the altar burn down, and handed me a ball of wax, saying "I'm going to bed now, Mommy. Wake me when my brother is born." Two hours later, the ball of wax broke in my hands. As it did, my water broke. That labor was all of two hours.

In the case of my own children, performing an actual ritual for myself was the farthest thing from my mind. But when the labors were over and I held my babies, I drew a pentagram on their foreheads, and said, "Welcome to my family's Circle. May you be watched over by the God and Goddess, and may each day bring you new joy and learning."

There is a lovely German birthing custom. When the father cuts the umbilical cord, he bends down to the baby and breathes into its mouth, saying, "I give you the breath of life. Welcome to our family."

There was one additional step. For my daughter it was something that I performed; for my son, it was performed by Kenny. After the pentagram was drawn, I whispered a name in my daughter's ear. This is her "secret" name, one that is only spoken at very special moments. The name given is given in blessing and hope. It asks the blessing of the namesake, and the hope that those attributes will be bestowed on the child. For my son, Kenny whispered a name after giving the first breath.

As my daughter has grown, I have whispered this name in her ear during times of stress or fear. Each time the magick has worked and she has been calmed and soothed. The name is never spoken aloud, and should she later decide to remain on this spiritual path, as mother I will offer her the choice to use this name publicly. There is a very strong bond between us, as we are the only two people who know this name. The same applies to my son and husband. We honor the silence, and never try to play twenty questions to guess those names. Some things really are best left unspoken.

Once these simple rituals are performed there is no reason for the parent to feel compelled to do anything else at the time of the birth. The labor and delivery are usually hectic and emotional, no matter how well you plan them. Birthing is a magickal act, and casting a Circle can keep one from noticing the magick that's happening there all by itself.

Most hospitals allow the placenta to be kept by the family. Mention it to the birthing staff, and they will put it in a bucket for you. There are some people who choose to eat the placenta. Many women do this as a way to replace a good deal of the iron that is lost during the birth. Many vegetarians will eat the placenta because nothing must die in order for this meat to be available. This may seem a bit too much for others. The placenta is, however, a magickal object. It bound one life to another, then went through its own birth when neither mother nor child needed it any longer. A placenta ritual is a very good way of celebrating the shift from pregnancy to parenthood.

RITUAL FOR BURYING THE PLACENTA

A very old folk custom in the British Isles involved taking the placenta to the village grove. The British have always been reverent of the magick and longevity of trees, and bonds are formed with trees during many British Rites of Passage rituals. The Yule tree and the Maypole represent sacred trees (see the discussion of Puberty Rites). The Morris dance, a sacred fertility rite, is done with sticks made of saplings. Most old English villages have a grove of trees where families have special trees and where rites like this are performed. In the grove, a hole would be dug and the placenta would be placed into the Earth and a sapling planted over it. This formed a bond between the child and the growing tree. Later, when the child's first nail clippings were taken, the tree would be the site of a subsequent ritual, the Gift of Song ritual.

If this has been a winter birth, you may choose to wait until the spring to perform this ritual. All that needs to be done is to place the placenta in the freezer. Likewise, if the mother wants to wait until after her bleeding has ceased, you can freeze the placenta. There is no "right time" to perform this ritual. It can be performed whenever it suits the family.

Various methods can be used to determine the type of tree to plant atop the placenta. Some may use divination, perhaps the *Celtic Tree Oracle,* or a Runic system. (There aren't exact correlations between runes and trees, although many of the qualities can be easily inferred.) In Celtic and German mythologies, trees are associated with various Gods and Goddesses. You may simply use intuition, or a tree under which you like to sit. You may choose your family's favorite tree. There is a good deal written about trees in *The White Goddess* by Robert Graves and this may be a good guide for selecting a tree. If this is the case, one needs to take into account that not all trees will grow in all climates. You should check with your local nursery to find out, for instance, whether rowan or alder will grow in your area.

Once the tree is chosen, or the sapling is ready to be replanted, you are ready to gather friends and family for the ritual. If you have chosen to plant a sapling, prepare the hole in which the tree is to be placed by carefully following the instructions of the nursery from which you purchased the tree. It will do no good to attempt to bond with this tree if it is not given the proper chance to grow. I would call this logical magick.

After the preparations for replanting the sapling are completed, family and friends should form a Circle around the planting site. If you have chosen an already grown tree, people should gather around it. You may chant as a preparation for the rite, or have a moment of silent hand holding. When the time feels right, the mother begins.

Mother: We are all children of the Earth. The Earth is
                 our Mother and we all draw life and prosper-
                 ity from Her.

Father: Our Mother's body is freely given to us in
                 love, so that we, Her children, may grow.
                 Our family has grown, and today we wish to
                 return to the Earth Mother that which
                 sustained our child.

Mother: From my womb, to the womb of the Mother.
                 (She places the placenta in the ground.) We
                 give thanks for life the greatest of all gifts.

Family and friends are now invited to place offerings and gifts
into the hole. It is suggested that these be biodegradable gifts
that will nurture the soil and the tree. Although the sentiment
of jewelry and such is welcomed, it would be better to concern
oneself with the care of the tree itself. Food, such as fruits and
honey, or plant food, might be appropriate. Also ceramic
items, such as tiny God and Goddess figures, would be a
wonderful gift, because ceramic (unglazed) is of the Earth.

When the sapling is placed in the ground above the
placenta, a watering can should be passed around the Circle.
Each member may speak a blessing for the family, or pledge
support of the family in some tangible way, as the new
member is nurtured and assimilated over the next few weeks.
When an existing tree is chosen the hole should be dug near
the base of the trunk, and perhaps bulbs should be planted as
gifts. As each member pours a little of the Water upon the
tree, he/she might say, "As I nurture this growing tree, so I
will nurture this growing family by . . ." and state their pledge.

The baby should be introduced to his/her tree. The parent
who whispered the name at birth may now choose to whisper
this name to the tree. As always, the singing of songs and

sharing of stories is encouraged. If the weather is warm, this should be done around the tree as food and drink is shared. After the food is shared some should be left nearby as a libation, but not necessarily under the tree itself raccoons, skunks and opossums could easily knock over the newly planted sapling.

If the tree is large enough to hold ribbons well, you may choose to decorate it, or to place small bells on the branches. The bells not only awaken the spirits, but will also serve to keep small animals away so that the tree has a chance to acclimate itself to the new location. If the family decides to bury the placenta under a tree already grown, it might be appropriate to hang a bird feeder from the branches as a special gift to the Mother's winged children. The group could even build a simple feeder, and tend it together. As the child grows, her/his special relationship with tree, birds, and bird feeder can be explained, and the child might join in caring for the feeder with the group.

RITUAL FOR RETURNING THE PLACENTA

Another traditional custom involved casting the placenta into a large body of Water—usually the ocean or a large lake—returning it to the Mother. Water has always been associated with the womb of the Goddess. The Celts symbolized the ocean as the cauldron of the primal Goddess, Cerridwen, and the Greeks told of Aphrodite, the embodiment of motherhood, rising from the salt waves. Circe lived on a Mediterranean island, and Isis created life each year in the Nile's flooding Waters. It is natural, then, that rituals centering around the Water have been created for the magick of birthing. Offerings of fruit and honey often accompanied the placenta in these rituals, which were reverent, joyous and celebratory. This is a ritual of giving thanks to the Mother of All, the Goddess, for the gift of giving life.

Like the preparations for burying the placenta, the timing of the ritual, and the particular body of Water should be determined by the family. Perhaps there is a favorite camping spot, or a lake house that has special memories and associations. It could be a pond or a nearby beach area that the family is well acquainted with, or a romantic spot visited on special occasions. Of course your geographic location will affect the ritual. If you live in Kansas, an ocean ritual is going to be difficult. Here again, logic may have to override romance.

The parents may choose to create a small litter to carry the placenta out to sea. A basket may be used for the same purpose. To carry my daughter's placenta out to sea, I baked a round sweet bread to hold the placenta, surrounded by offerings of fruit and honey. Family members and friends should also bring offerings, perhaps of fruit or small hand-made trinkets, to celebrate the return of the organ that provided life for the littlest family member.

With the placenta arrayed in its "boat," participants are invited to place their offerings alongside it. Depending on the number of celebrants, several "boats" may be necessary and you may find yourself creating these spontaneously from found natural objects. When all have made their offerings the parents, perhaps assisted by other family members, should lift this flotilla and bring it close to the shore or Waters' edge. Here everyone may join hands and form a semicircle around the family. Standing this way is a representation of the womb itself. You may wish to take a few moments to meditate or to chant to help set the ritual mood. When the moment feels right, the mother begins.

Mother: My womb has known the mystery of birth.
               The sea is womb of our Mother, life has
               always flowed from here. We are all born of
               these Waters that flow from the Mother.

Father: These Waters flow endlessly, as love flows
            within our lives. Today, in love, we return
            this gift to our Mother, and continue the
            cycle of life.

Mother: Thank you Mother of us all.

The mother or father may wish to draw a pentagram on the forehead of the baby with some Water, and whisper the child's name in her/his ear. A small jar of the Water from the lake or ocean might be collected and placed on a shrine in the baby's room, to be used in the upcoming Wicanning (naming) ritual.

There should be a few moments of silence at the end of the ritual, during which the group shares the last glimpse of their offering floating out to sea. When the boat can no longer be seen, it is time to leave the ritual area. When an offering is made to the sea, one should never look back in curiosity because it is considered rude to view the Water spirits, or undines, as they carry the food away. Stories and feasting may take place further away, where family and guests may be comfortably out of view of the ritual area.

You may visit this ritual site often as the child grows, and encourage her/him to learn to swim in these Waters, and to take care of the waterfront area. Teaching the child about the special bond she/he has with this sacred site is one way in which your family can share everyday magick.

FIRST WEEKS OF LIFE

At no time in a person's life do things change as rapidly and with as much permanence as they do in the first few weeks of life. As we watch, each day brings a new triumph for the baby. Every new skill is marvelled over and shown off by the proud parents. Phone calls herald the news: "She rolled over by herself," "I think he smiled at me!" These are all Rites of Passage. Attention should be paid to each one, perhaps recorded in a journal. (That's why Hallmark sells so many baby record books.) We have a need to remember, a need to celebrate, and an unspoken need for ritual.

Today, much of the focus is on the baby, not the parents. It must be noted that each skill that a child masters, empowers him/her and removes something from the parents. It is natural for parents to become depressed, to feel a little out of control and maybe even to feel a little bitter. While rituals themselves may not entirely remove these feelings, they can help to put the transitions into perspective. If you learn to regard these changes and triumphs as gifts, as milestones, then a different light is shed upon them. It would be tempting to include something about each change here, but then we also run the risk of over-emphasizing ritual and forgetting that magick is in the experience of everyday life.

Along with the progress that the baby makes daily, there are myriad new skills required of the parents, and these are not often discussed in the reference books about babies. Cutting the baby's nails for the first time is one of these. To reclaim the significance of this event, we shall look to an old European custom called "The Gift of Song."

After the baby's nails have been cut for the first time, they should be saved in a small piece of fabric. They must then be taken to a special tree, perhaps where the placenta was buried. A very small hole is dug at the base of the tree; and the nails are placed in the hole, along with offerings to the tree. Those gathered there speak to the spirit of the tree and ask that the child be given a gift of song, or a similar blessing. My friends asked that my children be gifted with lyrical voices, to speak well of other people, to sing well, and to possess eloquence. One rather wise friend asked also for a gift of silence, so that they might hear their own inner voices.

Later, as the child grows, visit the tree with her/him often, and tell the story of how this simple ritual was performed. Teach the child songs while sitting under the branches of the tree, and introduce the child to meditation there.

POSTPARTUM RITES

Many people will try to go on with "life as normal" after their baby is born. In our society, where self-reliance is so prized, this is almost expected. The impact of a first child on the family structure can be difficult and isolating. This is especially true if a couple has been accustomed to traveling, entertaining, performing rituals regularly, or other social events. They may find that many of their friends and family are suddenly less able to call spontaneously to suggest an activity. Some friends called me a few weeks after the birth of my daughter, inviting me out to a movie. As I put on my coat and was walking out the door, I said to myself, "Wait, I have a baby!" The reality of having this little person in my life struck home at that moment.

Much has been said about postpartum blues as they affect the mother, yet both parents are at a very real risk of becoming lost as individuals after the baby is born. The mother received a great deal of attention during her pregnancy. With the baby here, many friends and relatives will offer support to the mother while she is nursing and nurturing. The father is often overlooked as a primary care-giver even though traditional roles within the family have shifted. He also is going through the uncertainty of a changing family dynamic, as well as all-night colic and dirty diapers. When our son was an infant, Kenny was the primary baby comforter because no babysitter, either family or friends, could stop Jesse from crying until Daddy came home. This caused a lot of anxiety for Kenny, who felt guilty every time we left our son with a sitter, especially if it was a friend. Family wasn't as bad; the worst they could do was to refuse to babysit again until Jesse was seventeen or so.

There are rituals that can be viewed as a way to end the pregnancy phase, and to integrate the new person into the family structure. A Wiccaning, or naming ritual, is a way to fully welcome the baby. While this is a great moment of pride for the parents and family, the focus is still on the newborn. We need to take time for both mother and father to feel special, and to be acknowledged as the unique individuals that they are.

The rite for the mother is different in nature and feel from the father's, yet there are many overlapping elements. I will discuss these rites as if performed with only women and only men, but many couples will want to be present to support each other. When that occurs, the feelings of the parents must over-ride other concerns.

NEW MOTHERHOOD

The mother should allow her body to complete all postpartum bleeding before this rite is performed. There are several reasons for this. First, the womb is still healing and should be allowed to fully recover from the initial shock of the birthing, before the mother enters into a magickal atmosphere. Another factor is that sexual relations are generally discouraged until the bleeding has ended, and this rite is designed to reunite the couple as lovers in addition to being new parents. A more practical reason is that, for a little while, most women are still tired and caught up in the initial impact of caring for the baby. It may take a few weeks before a woman feels up to being involved with the Circle. The end of the bleeding period will often coincide with the desire to go back to activities that have been neglected since the birth.

While there are no hard and fast rules for the timing of the rite, the way in which the proper time is determined is important. I have known women who preferred to wait until the first full Moon postpartum, regardless of the flow of blood. In the tradition with which I am most familiar, there would be a period of one full week without bleeding before the rite was performed. This gives some extra time for both mother and child to adjust to the new life. If the mother has chosen to nurse, by now she will have gained some confidence and will be feeling more comfortable with this new role. There is also a chance that the bleeding may reappear, but if a full week passes with no blood one can be reasonably sure that it is, in fact, done.

This is a time in the family dynamic when the mother may be experiencing postpartum blues. If this is so, it may be better for the family or friends to suggest this ritual. Some new mothers are so caught up in caring for their babies that they lose sight of their own needs. By arranging the Circle for the mother, she is given the clear message that she is loved and missed, and that the time has come for her to be back. As long as trust bonds the Circle together, any method that brings the new mother back to ritual is the right way. Just bear in mind that this is a time of strange and unusual mood swings for most women, so any coaxing must be done with love and respect.

For this ritual, you will need one yard each of white, green and purple ribbons, and white, green and purple candles, if desired.

The Bath

Mix a bath wash of several drops of lotus oil in a pitcher of warm Water. Fill the tub with warm Water, then add jasmine leaves, rose petals, carnation oil and sea salt. As these items are added, say:

Fragrant leaves to conjure peace of mind.
Soft petals for the kiss of love.
Sweet oil to soothe and heal.
A gift from the sea, where all life began.

Burn the candles in the room if you wish. Help the mother
into the bath. Allow her to relax and to enjoy the feel of the
warm Water. The bath is a very womb-like experience, so it is
particularly fitting for this ritual.

After the mother has had a few minutes to herself, a woman
who has already borne children should come into the bath
and pour the herbal wash over her, saying:

> We honor you as Mother, for you have
> known the mystery of birth and the mystery
> of death. We welcome you as Sister, to join
> all of those who have borne as you have,
> shared your joys and felt your pains. We
> greet you as Friend, for the bonds we share
> are never broken. Blessed be.

The companion might stay with the mother a little while,
help her bathe, and discuss her feelings toward re-entering
the Circle. The companion should then help the mother
out of the tub, and dry her. Ideally, there will be several
women present to assist in the task. It is important that all
of these actions be carried out with love and respect for the
new mother. She must be nurtured, as she has been
nurturing her baby.

The Ritual

Bring the mother into the ritual space, and encourage her to recline on a cushion or a cot. Bring the candles from the bath into the ritual space.

A young woman or girl should represent the Maiden aspect of the Goddess, and a woman past her child-bearing years should represent the Crone. You may choose to have the parts acted out by three women who have had children.

Maiden: *(Laying the white ribbon across the mother's belly.)* I am Maiden. I was the secret you carried inside you in the beginning, when you belonged only to yourself. Long before you could feel life inside your womb, and long before others would look upon you and know, it was I who danced lightly in your heart. When you dreamed your dreams of youth and renewal, it was I who was there to dream with you. Though I have changed, I have never left you.

Mother: *(Laying the green ribbon across the mother's belly.)* I am Mother. When the life inside you was growing, and you began to feel it stir, I was there. As all the world watched and tried to feel with you the mystery of new life, I whispered in your ears and helped to comfort your deepest fears. My kiss placed a gentle blush on your cheeks, and my hand held yours when the child within cried out. Time has passed, and now you know me in yet another form. I have never left you.

Crone: *(Laying the purple ribbon across the mother's belly.)* I am Crone. As your time approached, it was I who helped to prepare you. My strength sustained you as the wheel turned on. In order for you to understand the beginning, I taught you about the ending. As your grandmothers before have always been midwives to their daughters and granddaughters, I stood by you. Slowly you came to understand that for your child to be born, a child inside of you must give way. I allowed you to cut your own cords to your past, as your child's cord was cut when new life began. Though I have done my job, I wait for you in dreams. I have never left you.

Maiden, Mother and Crone place their hands on the mother's belly.

All three: We have never left you. We have been with you from the beginning, and will be within you always.

Now all present hug the mother. After this, participants are encouraged to share a story about the pregnancy, about the mother herself, or about their own parenting experience. There should be food and drink for all to share.

When everyone has finished, the ribbons may be braided or otherwise saved. I used the same ribbons for both my daughter and son, and hope someday my daughter will use them when she is given this ritual.

NEW FATHERHOOD

Daddies have babies too. While it is true that they don't have morning sickness or experience labor pains, they experience a nine month pregnancy. Our men are often locked out of this wonderful time, or they get lost in the shuffle of family and friends' concern.

Imagine. His most intimate friend has gone through this amazing transformation beside him, day after day, night after night. He has watched as the Goddess revealed one of the most sacred mysteries, and all because of the part he played as lover! Why then is there little or nothing written about this? For too long our society has ignored the nurturing, caring male.

This has not always been the case. There was a time, not shrouded too deeply in archeological mystery, when men were honored for such qualities. Now is a good time to remember.

"Postpartum blues" is rarely used to describe what the new father is experiencing. Yet it happens. There needs to be more than just a roughhouse pat on the back and "I never knew you had it in you," to mark this change. I think that passing out cigars falls short of the mark as well.

The experience for men can be subtle and understated. Women bleed and then stop. There is an obvious beginning, middle and end. For the new father, a careful eye is needed. His feelings are real, but often are hard to discern in light of the attention being given to his partner. In this instance, the father is often very eager to take the role of principle support person for the woman who is most important to him. But just as often there is little support of this type for him.

In light of these potential difficulties, the timing of a ritual for new fatherhood needs careful consideration. If we are to give this rite full measure, allowing the father to feel his own importance, then it is not fair to time this ritual along with his partner's. If it happens to work that way spontaneously, it can be a lovely romantic notion, but it may be appropriate to separate them by weeks or even a month or two. This will help to give the new father the feeling that this is his ritual, not something done as a compliment to his partner's ritual simply to appease him.

If the family has buried the placenta under a tree, or if there is a favorite tree to which the father is drawn, this would be a good ritual site. During the winter months, there may be a strong leaning to work indoors. As with the timing, choosing the actual location should depend more on the nature and temperament of the father than on the possibly romanticized ideas of the other people involved.

The Ritual

The room or ritual space should be prepared and a small table should be used as an altar. A dark blue candle should be lit; a green and yellow candle should be ready, but not lit. Nuts or seeds should be placed on a plate, along with wine or juice, and ritual cakes.

The father should enter the ritual space first. He should be afforded a few moments to think over the events of the past year, and his new role as father.

Now a man who has already had children comes forward. He approaches the new father and says:

> Once, long ago, perhaps when you were still a
> child, you wondered, as we all have, about
> your grandfathers, your father, your children.
> Where in this great continuum did you stand?
> Like a star in the galaxy, crafted by the
> Mother, you wondered about the dizzying life

around you. Now, in the great pattern of life unending, you have mingled like the ivy into the vast mystery of the grandfathers. You have planted your seed, watched it grow, and witnessed your own immortality. For woman can bear life only by the seed of man, and man can be reborn only through woman. Today we honor you as Father, Brother and Friend. Blessed be.

Several men may wish to share the following parts. They need not be men who have fathered children, but they should be close to the new father. The names are meant only to evoke feelings, not necessarily to indicate the respective roles.

Youth:
The blue candle burns in front of you. It represents a time when you were unsure. Your emotions were deep and secret, hidden from the world and also from yourself. Today, we remember that time. This was your potential, for from those depths, those emotions, you shaped your own future. You responded to the call to life's renewal, even though you were unsure of yourself and burned with questions. These questions have grown and changed, but have never left you.

Dreamer:
(Lighting the green candle.) This is for the life you sired. Your dreams, your hopes, your seed, together became the beginning of a new life. The green of this candle reminds us of that. When you acted upon those unspoken desires, when you sought answers to those questions, when your love of life and your

belief in the continuation of life were awakened, your potentials became reality.

Father: *(Lighting the yellow candle.)* We light a yellow candle to remember the first light that shined upon your child. This was not just the light of the Sun, it was the light of the God: Lugh, Apollo, Taliesin. As your child was welcomed into this world, you must have known that a part of you, like the God, gave away life as a gift to life itself. For woman can bear only through the gift of your seed, and man can be reborn only through woman's gift of birth. So this is also the light of separation. As your child grows, you will watch yourself grow once again. Your child will look at the stars and will burn with questions. So this candle represents wisdom and promise. As the Sun rises each day, you will come to know that even long after you have gone on this child of yours will continue the great cycle.

Now the first man who entered the ritual space comes forward and blesses the wine/juice and cakes, and says:

This wine/juice is the fruit of life's labors. These cakes have grown from the Earth, and are a gift from our Mother. Both have felt the kiss of the Sun, a blessing from our Father. And in the name of the Father, these fruits gave life as a gift to life. Sharing these together, we nurture one another. Blessed be.

The drink and cakes are shared by all. This also is the time to share stories with each other, especially stories of fatherhood and parenting. When the time is right, the man who blessed the cakes will continue:

> These seeds and nuts are yours to take now. You have played a part in life's cycle. Keep these to remember always the promise of life's own renewal. But most important, remember that you must take time to renew yourself. We welcome you again as Friend, Brother and Father.

The father may now choose to keep the seeds or to plant them. They also may be saved and passed on to a son in later years.

There is one final step to these rituals, and that is to regain the balance of the couple as a couple. Whenever the rituals are over, the new parents should be allowed to take an evening for themselves. They need to feel reconnected as friends and lovers. They could be gifted with tickets to a show or a concert, or dinner reservations could be made for them at a favorite restaurant. Taking the baby out for an evening so that the couple can enjoy some time alone without worrying about the child would go a long way toward helping them to get over the "blues."

2

WICCANING

Even as the Great Goddess, the Mother of All Things gave
the gift of life to her Children, you too have understood those
mysteries. Now you must learn to allow that life to grow into
its own being and follow its own true nature. Just as the
Goddess Herself must let all things follow their paths, you
must allow your child to follow his or hers path.
> —from a traditional blessing

With the baby growing into its new family, and the parents completing their postpartum rituals, the initial adjustment period is quickly passing. Parents and child(ren) have settled into a daily routine. The family has spent time bonding, and the new roles are reasonably defined. Friends have (we hope) been supportive and helpful. This is the time for the parents to show thanks for the support given, and for continued support. It is a time of welcoming.

It is time for the Wiccaning, or naming ritual. This is a public statement of who the baby is, where she/he fits into the family structure, and a ritual of asking that the Gods and Goddesses bless the baby. It is performed among family and friends to publicly share thanks and support.

In the past, when the certainty of a child's survival was less certain, the Wiccaning may not have been held until a full year after the birth. In fact, there are no particular reasons for the ceremony to take place at this time, except that in our culture the "christening" or "baptism" ritual is done early on, and for many the Wiccaning serves a similar purpose. Indeed, the rituals of later religions are adapted from the Wiccan naming ritual, and baptism by Water was used in the naming ritual by many pre-Christian cultures, including Celts and Jews. There are of course major theological differences between the Wiccaning and a Christian baptism, but since so many of us feel connected with the rituals of our childhood there is a natural tendency to want to do *something,* and the intent of welcoming the new one into the spiritual and social community is the same in all of these.

We do not perform this ritual to promise our children to the Gods. This is not a bargain made to ensure their eternal well-being. A Wiccaning simply asks both the God and the Goddess and the Spirits of the Four Directions, to watch over and guide our children. As adults we have made a spiritual commitment. While we do not wish to force-feed spirituality to our children, there is a reason to give them a background, a starting point. By asking those Gods and Goddesses that we honor to guide those whom we love, we are merely placing our children in Their care until the children are old enough to make spiritual decisions for themselves. A Wiccaning means no more, no less. I have heard parents argue that Christian, Jewish or other spirituality was "forced down their throats" as children, and that this has made them uncomfortable teaching spirituality to their own children. But for many of them, even though this spirituality was not the one that they ultimately accepted and the way in which it was presented was perhaps inappropriate, it did give them the spiritual structure they needed to seek the path that they came to embrace. This is the best reason I can think of to raise a child in one's own spiritual path.

If, like many in today's world, you have found your spiritual path after your child has grown beyond the newborn stage, you can still use the Wiccaning ritual as a way to incorporate your child(ren) into the family's spiritual practice. It is an appropriate ritual for any child up to seven or eight years of age (after that age the dedication ritual may be more appropriate). The same applies to those who have adopted children into the family. As was true for the Conception Ritual, we are more concerned here actions and intent than with the mechanics of the ritual. The Wiccaning ritual is a good way to bring children into the family's beliefs, and is especially good for adopted children.

Every child is entitled to a larger family than just their biological parents. One of the important parts of the Wiccaning ritual includes having a woman and a man stand as the Goddessmother and Godfather of the child. Their job is multifaceted. Much more is involved here than just promising to take care of a child in the event that his/her parents are unable to do so. In this ritual, the adults agree to become involved fully with the child, an agreement that will span from babysitting and childcare to teaching, sharing, and listening. In this way we choose the members of our extended family and help to define some of the roles within that structure. For this reason, the Goddessmother and Godfather should ideally be close friends within the Circle, housemates, and/or good friends with similarly aged children.

There is one other part of this ritual that needs to be given additional thought. Many people have chosen a special name that represents something to aspire toward. At the birth of your child you may have whispered a secret name in the child's ear. The bestowing of a special public name is part of the Wiccaning ritual. Both parents should agree on the name, and at a given point in the ritual they should speak it for all to hear. Later, as the child grows, she/he will come to understand that this is a special name that is to be used only in the Circle. If there is a need to keep the Circle a "secret," the name will help to further emphasize that point. When choosing a name for a child, try to think of a name that will evoke a quality that you would wish the child to grow into, or one that denotes that the child is a part of the family. For instance, if a father's Circle name is Bran, then Gwern (Bran's son in the Bardic cycle *The Mabinogi*) is an excellent choice for the son. Or perhaps you have been blessed with a little girl with soft, gentle features. Then perhaps a name such as Fawn, or a floral name like Willow might be a good choice. Remember, this name can be changed as your child grows, particularly at the time of their dedication.

The Ritual

Friends and family gather together in the ritual place. Two members who have agreed to serve as the Priest and Priestess have arranged the altar, and those that have been given the honor of becoming Goddessparents stand inside the Circle. Parents and new baby stand inside the Circle alongside the Goddessparents. The room is decorated with flowers and ribbons. This is not only a ritual, but a celebration. There should be laughter and decorations to welcome this new child of the Goddess and God.

Sweeping

Sweeping is traditionally the privilege of the maiden, the youngest dedicated female. She begins in the East and sweeps the area three times deosil (clockwise). Those in the Circle visualize her clearing away all unwanted energy and thoughts. As she sweeps, the following words may be used.

Maiden: New families are a time of new beginnings.
            We sweep aside our expectations so that
            this child has freedom to grow in her (his)

own world. This Circle prepares the way for her (him) to experience life within our family, but not to be restricted by our boundaries. So the Circle is swept. Blessed be.

Casting the Circle

The Priestess will help to separate the Circle from the boundaries of the outside world, creating the sacred "space between the worlds" of people and deity. She may use a wand to cast the Circle. The wand might be made from a branch of the tree used in the placenta ritual, or in the Gift of Song rite.

Priestess: We cast this Circle to place ourselves between the worlds. May this space be a meeting place for ourselves and our Gods. As we cast this Circle, we join together within it to welcome (name) to our Circle and family. This Circle is formed in love. Blessed be.

Elemental Blessings

The purpose of the Wiccaning is to bring the family together within the Circle, and to renew the bonds of the extended family, the Circle or coven. In keeping with that idea the elements should be passed around the Circle, from one person to the next, allowing person one to invoke some aspect of each element. Beginning in the East, take the incense and pass it around the entire Circle. People may ask for "inspiration" or "clear thoughts," and so on. When the incense has gone around, repeat this process for Fire (red candle), Water and Earth (salt).

You may make an incense for Wiccaning. Use about equal parts of the following herbs: chamomile, rose petals, lavender and gum mastic. Blend well and add three drops of red wine and 1/4 teaspoon of honey. Allow to dry completely and burn over charcoal.

Calling the Quarters

Now that the Circle has been cast and blessed, we can invite the Quarters, or Spirits of the Four Directions, into the Circle. Here the parts are divided between the Priest, Priestess, and Goddessparents, to emphasize their special relationship with the newest family member.

Priest:	We welcome you, Spirits of East! You who are of childhood and beginnings, join our Circle and bring us the gifts of the morning light and the perfumed Air. Be welcomed here. Blessed be.
Godfather:	We welcome you, spirits of South! You who are of the joys of creating new life, join our Circle and bring us the warmth of the noon Sun and the fullness of summer's flowers. Be welcomed here. Blessed be.
Priestess:	We welcome you, Spirits of West! You who are the Waters where life begins, the Waters that nurture us all, join our Circle and bring to us the welcome shadows of dusk and caring as deep as the ocean. Be welcomed here. Blessed be.
Goddessmother:	We welcome you, Spirits of North! You who are the protectors of this tiny new one,

join our Circle and bring the beauty of the midnight sky and the promise of a new day. Be welcomed here. Blessed be.

Calling the Gods

With our Circle built, and the sacred space defined, we can now invite the Gods to be part of this ritual. The Priestess should invoke the Goddess, and the Priest should invoke the God (some groups do this in opposite order, with the Priestess invoking the God; others have one member invoke both Goddess and God). The handmaiden or the youngest girl should light a candle for the Goddess and one for the God as They are called.

Priestess: Earth Mother, Star Sister, Lady of myriad names and faces. We your children call to you. Join us in this Circle, and share in this rite. Blessed be.

Priest: Sky Father, Wind Brother, He whose name has been sung by wind in the trees since time's beginning. Join us in the Circle and share in this rite. Blessed be.

Priestess: This is a time of great happiness for our Circle family. Today, we will celebrate the Wiccaning of _____ and ask the blessings of the Four Directions and of the Goddess and God for this beloved child of our Circle. While we ask for Their blessings, we make no promise for this child. If, when _____ has grown older, she/he chooses to walk this path, then he/she will make their own

promise. For now, we ask only for guidance
and blessings.

The parents now bring the child to each of the quarters. In
each quarter they should hold the child facing outward as they
ask for the blessings.

East: Here is _____. We ask for the blessings of
an inquisitive mind, and a sense of good
humor. Watch over _____, and with
each new day teach him/her your mysteries.
So mote it be.

South: Here is _____. We ask for the blessings of
quick wit and strong will. Watch over
_____, and with each new day teach
him/her your mysteries. So mote it be.

West: Here is _____. We ask for the blessings
of great love and temperament. Watch over
_____ and with each new day teach him/
her your mysteries. So mote it be.

North: Here is _____. We ask for the blessings
of patience and strength. Watch over
_____, and with each new day teach
him/her your mysteries. So mote it be.

Parents return to the East for a moment, and then face the
center of the Circle and the God and Goddess candles asking
for Their blessings.

Together: God and Goddess, Ancient Ones, Earth
Mother and Sky Father. We ask that you

watch over _____, and help to guide
his/her steps along her/his own path.
Today we also ask that you hear his/her
new name with our Circle. Here is
(Circle name) . Bless and teach him/her
Your great mysteries each day. Blessed be.

Now the Goddessparents, those chosen by the family as
Goddessmother and Godfather, face the child to make their
promises. The words spoken should be carefully chosen, as
this is a special honor, and should not to be taken lightly. The
words included here are meant only as a guide, since each
family circumstance will be different.

Godfather: I have watched you grow from the time
                    you were inside your mother's womb, and
                    have awaited your arrival into our Circle.
                    Today, I have the honor of becoming a
                    special part of your life.

                    I promise to be there with you and your
                    parents as you grow, to help you, and to
                    share in the wonder of discovery with you.
                    I look forward to teaching you, but even
                    more, of looking at the world through your
                    eyes, and once again seeing magick around
                    me. Welcome to our family.

Goddessmother: I, too, have long awaited your arrival, and I
                    rejoiced with your mother when you were
                    born. There will be many times over the
                    years when you will want or need to be
                    with someone other than your own
                    mother. I am honored for the love and

54

trust that led your parents to name me your Goddessmother. I promise you that I will try to be patient and fair, and will always try to find the time to listen to what you are saying, and to the meaning beyond your words. I look forward to a time of mutual sharing and discovery as you come to understand the world around you. Welcome.

The Goddessparents may also choose to address the parents as well, to offer their support over the next few years. After they have finished speaking, it would now be appropriate for other members of the Circle to speak, if they wish. Circle members may also want to share memories or stories here.

Wine and Cakes

Sharing food and drink in a Circle is another way of thanking the Gods for the many gifts given us. Those who love each other provide for each other, so Wine and Cakes is also meant to underscore the feeling of family and community. The Priestess may hold the wine and the Priest may hold the cakes, or the parents may hold wine and cakes while the Priest and Priestess speak.

Priestess: This wine is a gift of the harvest. The fruits were nurtured by the Sun and kissed by the rain. As we drink, we taste the sweet offering of the grapes and remember the bounty bestowed by Her upon us. Blessed be.

Priest: These cakes are a gift from the Earth. We

share them as a family and remember all of
the Earth's children and, especially, our family
of friends and loved ones. As long as we are
alive and there is bounty in the Earth, let no
one of us ever want for either food or family.
Blessed be.

Closing the Circle

Before we leave the Circle, we take time to thank the Gods
and the four directions for Their presence.

Priestess: Earth Mother, Gentle One who guides all our
paths. We thank you for being here in our
Circle and for sharing in this ritual of naming.
As we extinguish these candles, we remember
that You always are a part of us. Blessed be.

Priest: Sky Father, Wise One who helps to guide our
steps. We thank you for being with us in our
ritual. Though we may extinguish these
candles, we look for your blessing each day, as
the Sun brings your light. Blessed be.

Now the Quarters are thanked. As each part is spoken,
members of the Circle kiss two fingers of their right hand and
hold them up to the direction named.

Priest: Spirits of East, we thank you for the gifts
that you have shared with us. We remem-
ber you each time a breeze touches our
face. As you return to your home, we leave
you with a kiss. Blessed be.

Godfather: Spirits of South, we thank you for the gifts

that you have brought and shared with us. Every time we feel the warmth of the Sun or a hug, we remember you. May you return home, with a kiss. Blessed be.

Priestess: Spirits of West, your gift of love has touched all of us here, for the promise of new beginnings has always been hidden in your depths. We thank you for being with us here, and we send you home with a kiss. Blessed be.

Goddessmother: Spirits of North, we thank you for being here in our Circle. Your gifts of security and stability will be remembered as we watch the stars appear each night. Now, as you return home, we thank you with a kiss. Blessed be.

Now we return the Circle once again to Earth. The Priestess walks around the Circle three times widdershins (counterclockwise) carrying a candle or athame.

Priestess: Though we end this Circle, the family gathered here will always share its warmth. The ritual has been completed, but the promises made are just begun. Merry meet, merry part and merry meet again. Blessed be.

FIRST STEPS

A newborn sees the world through its parents eyes. He or she relies entirely on his/her parents for food, input and play. The newborn's parents are its whole world. But with the passage of time, the child begins to develop the motor skills that allow it to explore the world for itself. Each day brings new accomplishments, and we witness the slow blossoming of an individual.

It would be hard to say exactly when a baby becomes its own person, but one milestone is the ability to take those first exploratory steps. In keeping with the notion that each milestone in a person's life should be celebrated, we have a ritual called "First Steps." This ritual celebrates the first glimpse of independence and individuality. It is a simple ritual, one that may be meaningful to the parents and to the extended family, but one that is also understood by the child.

In addition to both parents, the Goddessparents and the Circle or extended family should be present. This is a statement to child, parents and Circle that the child is now accepted as an individual within the group. Because of the uniqueness of this ritual, there are several special considerations for the setup.

Arrange the altar with your family's favorite tools. In each quarter you will need to place herbs or flowers for the child to walk on (chamomile and daisies for the East, cinnamon and roses for the South, carnations and cornflowers for the West, and pine and moss for the North). Have a small pouch ready to collect some of each herb after the ritual. The focus of this ritual is the child, so this ritual reflects consideration for the child's taste in food and drink. It is a good idea to place cookies or fruit on the altar in a place where the child will be able to see them. The chalice should contain a favorite drink for the child.

There are also parts of the ritual that call for gifts to be presented to the child. This is a very basic way of assuring the child that he/she is loved and cared for, a way that all children understand. These gifts will be especially meaningful if they come from members of the Circle and not just from the immediate family. This is also a way for the members of the Circle to show their love and commitment to the child on this special occasion.

Prepare the child by telling him/her about the ritual throughout the day. Explain how excited and proud you are feeling. Tell him/her that tonight, he/she is going to walk to the altar by him/herself to show everyone how much he/she has grown, and to show the God and Goddess that he/she wants to be part of the Circle.

It is not necessary to take a special bath, unless it is customary for the family to do so before the ritual. Family and guests should be encouraged to wear special robes to celebrate, perhaps something more childlike or festive than usual. This would be a good time to present the child with a new robe.

You can make a special incense for this ritual. Use equal parts of the following: woodruff leaves, chamomile, lavender and rose petals. Add to a mix of one part frankincense and one part sandalwood powder. Mix, and add a drop of pine oil to the herbs. Burn on charcoal.

The ritual calls for annointing the child. Mix together equal parts of carnation oil and light musk oil. Add 1/8 part vetivert oil. If the oils that you are using are uncut, mix into a light natural oil such as apricot.

The Ritual

All assemble to cast the Circle, except for the mother and the child. They wait outside of the ritual area, perhaps watching the ritual and discussing the casting being done for the child's special Circle. The mother now places socks with circular holes cut in the bottom of them on the child's feet. These signify that the child is still nurtured (clothed), but becoming an individual with his/her own feet touching the ground.

Sweeping the Circle

All, except mother and child, assemble in the ritual area. The altar is in the center, as always. The maiden begins to sweep the Circle three times, beginning in the East. (The spoken parts given here are to show intent, and can certainly be altered to conform to the needs and vocabulary of the members of the Circle).

Maiden: *(Sweeping the Circle.)* This is a time of growing, and welcoming. With this besom (broom) we clear away all trace of false and uncertain steps. Here we make way for surety and the confidence that comes with growth. With each step that we take to cleanse this Circle, may we find renewed strength and purpose.

Mixing Salt and Water

Using an athame (knife) or similar tool, the Priestess mixes a bit of salt into the Water.

Priestess: All life begins in the Water, all emotion stems from here as well. Let this Water be cleansed of all doubts and fears *(here she removes three drops of Water)* and be blessed with security and pleasure. *(Here she may draw a penta-gram in the Water.)*

Salt is the symbol of foundation and stability. Let this salt be blessed, for we wish each step to be firm and surefooted.

(Adding three measures of salt to the Water.)
As we would blend our love with our
strength, so we mix this salt and Water. This
union is blessed here and now as it has been
blessed by our ancestors before us. Blessed
be.

Casting the Circle

The Priestess may use a wand for the Circle casting. I would
suggest a wand of willow wood. She should walk around the
Circle three times deosil.

Priestess: This Circle is cast out of love for each other
and for the Goddess and God. Let this space
be apart from the world, and remain within
the world, in which we live. Here we gather
to celebrate the growing and changing of
(name)   , to welcome him/her to our Circle.

Elemental Blessings

The elements are carried around the Circle, beginning in the
East, by the Priest or various members of the family/Circle as
they ask for Their blessings.

Priest: *(Carrying incense.)* This is sweet Air, the
breath of the Gods. Let this Air bring renewed inspiration to our Circle and childlike
visions to all here.

A candle to represent Fire is brought around the Circle in the
same manner.

Priest: *(Carrying candle.)* The light from this candle allows us to walk during both day and night with equal confidence. Let this candle remind us to take each step without fear and with purpose.

A bowl of Water is brought around, and Water is gently sprinkled around the Circle.

Priest: *(Carrying water.)* It is the love of the Goddess, our Mother, that washes away all fears. Where this Water falls, let no fear remain, nor sadness linger.

A bowl with salt is brought around, and salt is placed along the perimeter of the Circle.

Priest: *(Carrying salt.)* A promise was made when this life began, to nurture and to protect the new life. This salt reminds us that all promises must be honored. We gladly remember and honor this promise tonight.

Calling the Quarters

Each quarter is called into the Circle to bring its unique gifts. It is nice to have each quarter invited by a different member of the Circle as a way to demonstrate to the child that *all* involved are an important part of his/her life.

East: Spirits of East, welcome! Join us here as the butterfly in flight. Come to us as the gentle breeze of spring and the soft scent of flowers. Be a part of every breath and every word

spoken here. Spirits of East, be welcomed.
Blessed be.

South: Spirits of South, welcome! Join us here at the
dancing hearth Fire. Come as the warmth of
the summer's Sun and the brightness of
children's eyes. Be a part of every song and
every hug shared here. Spirits of South, be
welcomed. Blessed be.

West: Spirits of West, welcome! Join us here as a
babbling brook, ever searching, ever singing.
Come to us as the rain falls to give new life to
the Earth below. Be a part of every drink
shared here in love and joy. Spirits of the
West, be welcomed. Blessed be.

North: Spirits of North, welcome! Join us as the
trees stand against the night sky. Come as the
firm hand that guides each of our steps. Be a
part of every action taken here. Spirits of the
North, be welcomed. Blessed be.

Calling the Gods

After the Circle is complete, we invite the Gods to join us.
The Priestess may call the Goddess, the Priest may call the
God.

Priestess: Gentle Mother, we call you. Join us in our
Circle to share the new dance of _____.
Be a part of all of dances, now and always.

Priest: Gentle Father, we call you. Join us in our

Circle to share the strength and growth of
_____ . Be a part of all gathered here,
now and always.

Priestess: We are gathered here tonight to celebrate the
First Steps of _____. We prepare
now to welcome him/her to our Circle.

Now both mother and child are summoned to the northeastern edge of the Circle.

Mother: When I birthed you, I promised to care for
you and to love you. The night of your
Wiccaning I asked the Gods and Goddesses
to watch over you, and to guide and
protect you. Now you have grown enough
to walk in your own steps. These socks are
a gift from me. The holes in the bottoms
remind all of us that, even though you will
only be my child for a short time, you will
ever be a child of Mother Earth.

At this point the mother shows the child the altar and he/she is encouraged to walk to the altar alone. (It is often necessary to "assist" by making those cookies real obvious.) The Goddessparents greet the child.

Goddessmother: Welcome home. We are all so proud of
you and happy tonight.

Godfather: Tonight you have taken your first steps
alone in our Circle. We hope that it is the
first of many times that you will join us.

Goddessmother: Now we will walk the Circle and you will
have a chance to meet each Quarter.

They walk him/her to the East.

Godfather: Here is the East. The Spirits of the Air are
your friends. Think of the East as you walk
on daisies and chamomile, flowers of youth
and sweetness. The Air has given you
breath and the sense of wonder. May you
always be friends and grow together.
Blessed be.

You may decide to give the child a small gift of the East, such
as a pinwheel. Next they walk to the South.

Godfather: Here is the South. The Spirits of the South
are your friends. Think of the South when
you eat cinnamon, or smell roses, herbs
and flowers of strength and love. The Fire
has given you purpose and strong feelings.
May you always be friends and grow
together. Blessed be.

You may give a gift of the South, such as gingersnap cookies.
Next they walk to the West.

Goddessmother: Here is the West. The Spirits of the West
are your friends. Think of the West as you
see or smell carnation and cornflowers,
flowers of cleansing and love. The Water
has given you intuition and compassion.
May you always be friends and grow
together. Blessed be.

You may give a gift, such as a new bath toy. Next they walk to the North.

Goddessmother: Here is the North. The Spirits of the North are your friends. In the North there are pine and moss, both gifts from the forest floor. The North has given you a foundation, and will give you wisdom. May you always be friends and grow together. Blessed be.

You may give a gift of a small plant.

Godfather: See the candles burning? They represent the God and Goddess. Those flames remind us that They are always with us, here in the Circle, and everywhere. You will be our Goddesschild for a short time, but for your whole life you will be a child of the God and Goddess. They will always love you.

Goddessmother: The oil that I am placing on your brow is a kiss from the God and Goddess. *(She anoints the child's forehead.)*

The Goddessparents take the child to stand in front of the father, completing the Circle that was begun when the child was brought into the ritual by the mother. Father and mother (or co-parents) should be standing together.

Godfather: Here is your Father. It was his gift of love that led to your life's beginning. You will find, as you grow, that there is much about

love that you can learn together. May you
always be friends and grow with each other.
(Parents kiss each other, then kiss the child.)

At this point, the parents may have special words for their
child. If there are older siblings, they, too, may have words or
gifts. The Circle is open for sharing and for stories.

Wine and Cakes

The "wine" should be a favorite drink for the child and the
cookies or fruits should be a special treat. Mother and Father
should be given the honor of blessing the food, and the
children present should be allowed to bring it around the
Circle for sharing. Then, the Mother holds the cup and the
Father holds the cakes.

Mother: This drink is a gift from the Sky Father and
the Earth Mother. As the fruits grew they
were kissed by the rain and smiled on by the
Sun and the Moon. We share this tonight to
remember that we, too, are blessed by the
God and the Goddess, by the rain, the Sun
and the Moon. Blessed be.

Father: These cookies/fruits grew out of Mother
Earth. Father Sun watched over them. Now
they will feed us as the God and Goddess have
always fed our hearts and spirits. Blessed be.

Closing The Circle

Before we close the Circle we thank the Gods for joining us.

Priestess: Gentle Mother, we thank you for joining our Circle and celebrating with us tonight. We ask that Your blessing of love and nurturing remain in all of our hearts. As you leave for your home, we send you a kiss. *(Kisses two fingers, and holds them toward candle. The Goddess candle is extinguished.)*

Priest: Gentle Father, we thank you for joining our Circle and sharing in our pride of_____. We ask that Your blessing of protection and kindness remain in all of our hearts. As you leave for your home, we send you a kiss. *(God candle is extinguished.)*

The Quarters are now asked to leave by the same people who brought them into the ritual.

East: Spirits of East. Many thanks for your gift of soft words and words of kindness. As you leave now for your home, we send you a kiss.

South: Spirits of South. Many thanks for your gift of song and love. As you leave for your home, we send you a kiss.

West: Spirits of West. Many thanks for your gift of movement and joy. As you leave for your home, we send you a kiss.

North: Spirits of North. Many thanks for your gift of guidance and learning. As you leave for your home, we send you a kiss.

The Circle itself is now sent back to the Earth. Three times the Priestess walks widdershins around the Circle.

Priestess: This Circle is open, but never broken. We send it back to Mother Earth until we need to call on it again. Though we end this Circle, each time we gather together to celebrate we will return to this place that we share between the worlds. Merry meet, merry part, and merry meet again. Blessed be.

THE MAGICKAL YEARS OF WHY? AND (K)NO(W)

Up to now we have discussed rituals that celebrate the beginning of our child's journey through life. But our celebrations involve more than just rituals. Our way of life should celebrate each day as special and sacred. The next few years in the child's life are a time of endless questions, discoveries and magick. Many baby books will warn of the so-called "terrible twos," and how difficult they are. While there are no magick wands or spells to dispel some of the daily challenges of this age, this is a blessed time. It is important at this time in a child's life to celebrate achievements, and to keep the emotional impact of power struggles to a minimum.

We owe the sharing of our special beliefs to our children. More than that, if Mommy and Daddy do rituals and the children are not involved, we have often found that the children begin to feel "I'm not good enough to be in Mommy's religion." We in the Craft have embraced the strong, gentle, loving way of both a Goddess and God, which will nurture our children and give them the spirituality and tolerance to someday make responsible decisions on their own.

Incorporating small children into daily or even weekly rituals requires a steady and patient approach. In many religions and cultures around the world, small children are allowed to run freely while the adults pray. In other religious groups, the presence of children is discouraged, unless they are well enough behaved to qualify as vegetation. While not going to either extreme, there is much to be said for having a few toys tucked away in the ritual space to keep the youngest members of the Circle occupied. As they grow older, and more skillful, children might be encouraged to sweep the Circle or to put out candles, carry the cakes around, or other simple ritual acts. This gives our young ones the clear message that the Circle is a place where they are welcomed and cherished. Adding more hand holding, chanting, storytelling and dancing will make ritual a time that is looked forward to eagerly. Remember that each time a child is given a new responsibility in the Circle, or at home, it is a Rite of Passage for them. Remind them often that now they are older and can do more, not just for themselves, but for the entire family. Stressing this helps to demonstrate in real life what is talked about in our rituals.

It is important to try to be aware of the larger needs of the family structure. While it is more expedient and less messy to do many things for our children, rather than asking them to do these things themselves, especially in a ritual setting, we need to keep the children actively involved. If we are aware that each day offers a new beginning, both to our children and to ourselves, we allow the daily presence of magick to shine through. So many new skills are being worked on in these early years that it becomes a full-time occupation to keep track of them. A weekly journal kept during childhood would be a welcome reminiscence later on in our children's lives. It is possible to approach journal-keeping as a magickal act. Involve the child by keeping handprints, drawings, photos and found objects in the journal. Nature walks and walks through the park are perfect ways to teach the love of the Goddess and God, and provide a chance to do journal work together. This will also prepare the toddler or preschooler to visualize later learning as a magickal act.

Rather than approaching the toddler and preschool years as chapters in the baby care books, try to bear in mind that we are building memories for our children and ourselves. If we live a magickal life that includes our children, their memories will be magickal. Celebrating each new skill, from potty training to the ability to get food for themselves, strengthens magickal bonds. Acknowledging each new skill with a small, unstructured ritual is nice. It would be appropriate to add a special object, like a stone, to a shrine that was created together each time the child accomplishes something. This may help the child to see each accomplishment not as an added responsibility, but as a magickal achievement.

If we can work toward incorporating magick into our families' lives, and teach our children and ourselves the respect and integrity that comes with this lifestyle, then we will have begun to work on the greatest of all magickal acts. For it is our challenge to live each day as a unique opportunity to enact rebirth, as in a sacred Circle. With every rising of the Sun we see the wonder around us, and find new ways to grow within that wonder. What more appropriate way to teach magick than to begin here, with the initial stages of life?

3

THE AGE OF REASON

See how the world stretches out before you. When you first opened your eyes, great mysteries unfolded before you. Now, as your mind opens to accept more knowledge, the mysteries are greater still and the rewards are that much sweeter. Each time the Sun and the Moon complete a round of their celestial dance, each turning of the wheel will reveal to you more and more. Mark those passings with a smile, and learn to welcome their changes.

—family blessing for a child

New-found independence is a welcome transition, both to the child and to the family. During the school years, we aim towards expanding our childrens' minds and experiences as well as our own. Growth and physical maturity make many more things possible and new horizons open as never before. The child who was a little baby only a short time ago has found full voice and will. We become increasingly aware of one another's needs, and rationale. We have entered the Age of Reason.

From the first day of school until the onset of puberty, we will look at each other through ever changing, ever re-evaluating eyes. Behaviors that were acceptable in a three-year-old become intolerable in a five-year-old. Our roles within the family change quickly, and we look for ways to accommodate the people we are all becoming. With the beginning of school and new socialization, we need to find a way to maintain the spiritual balance that we worked so hard to establish in the beginning years.

This will be a time of many firsts for both parents and children. Our rituals must now fit into the ever increasing social schedule of our children. Many parents skittishly avoid "force-feeding" a spiritual path to their children not realizing that the alternative, not offering something spiritual, is abysmal. Children have many questions about the world around them and, as we know, our path helps to put many of those questions into perspective. The Age of Reason is a unique time to harness the natural magick found in our children's inquisitive minds. By teaching them about the magick found in many cultures and many paths, we set the stage for choices in later years. By stressing common features between spiritual and cultural viewpoints, we allow for a more holistic world view later in life. There will be ample time for our children to decide which, if any, path to follow. By building memories of magick and beauty, whatever path they eventually choose will be enriched.

LEARNING IS SWEET

I was raised in a Jewish family in which education was highly valued. I suppose it's a part of that cultural heritage. Long before I began school, I was told stories of one-room schoolhouses, called Cheders, where children would gather around a Rabbi, their teacher, to listen to their lessons. Images of round-cheeked and bright eyed-children looking into wise eyes haunted me as I approached my first day of school.

Going to school, leaving the safety of one's family and accepting teaching and instruction from a total stranger, is perhaps one of the most frightening things we ask our children to face. After five years of the family being our child's whole universe, we thrust our children into an uncertain place for which no amount of *Sesame Street* can prepare them. Even if they've had a pre-school experience, or some form of day care, there is nothing that can compare with the sheer size and child-swarming of a public school. This is a Rite of Passage that is universally recognized in our society, yet all that is done to mark it is to acquire a new pencil case or a lunch-box with cartoon turtles drawn on the sides.

In our family, a simple but significant ritual was observed to make that first school morning special for me. It was a way of making learning real. After the excitement of dressing in new school clothes and saying goodbye to childhood companions, Mamma took me to the schoolyard. I don't recall ever having seen that many children in one place before. There was a special yard for the kindergarten classes, and it was filled with the noise of excited children and the uncertain talk of nervous parents. Other mothers spoke in hushed tones and looked around the yard anxiously, but not mine. My mother stood there calmly, offering me a reassuring smile and squeezing my hand lovingly.

Someone blew a whistle, and magickally children formed lines. Our parents were invited to walk with us to our classrooms. As we entered the building my mother leaned over to me and said, "Remember the Cheder? This is just like that, only bigger. Grandma would be proud of you today." Visions of my grandmother rushed into my mind, and I felt her with me. She was once a little girl, just like me. I was certain that she had been brave when she had gone to school.

We finally arrived at the classroom. Children cried as their parents left them at the door. I looked at my mother. Her face broke into a smile. She said, "Open your mouth." I did as she told me, and something magickal happened. A drop of honey was placed on my tongue. "Learning is sweet," she whispered to me.
"Always remember that."

I walked into my classroom, tasting the honey on my tongue and remembering my grandmother. To say that I realized that this was an old tradition would not be true. But somewhere deep inside, where the magick really counts, I knew. I knew that for generations children had been given honey and had been told that learning is sweet. I knew that my mother, her mother, and her mother's mother had tasted honey as I did, and that the taste removed the fear.

Later, as I learned letters, Mamma baked letter-shaped honey cakes. As I identified each letter, I was given a cake in its shape. Learning indeed became something sweet.

When my own daughter stood in a schoolyard for the very first time, I had honey in my pocket. I looked into her blue eyes as she steadied herself to face the immense building with its crowded corridors. She looked up at me with eyes questioning, "Is it safe Mamma? Are you sure its really OK for me to go in there?" I smiled back at her and, just as my own mother had done, I placed a drop of honey on her tongue. Someday, my grandchildren will know.

My children are now being educated at home. For my son, there was never a time of standing at the threshold of a strange building. For him, the introduction to learning came from bright new books and clean white sheets of paper waiting to be created upon. As we sat down together for the first time, to change the dynamics of our relationship, I smiled at him. Once again the honey appeared, and a tradition that had been handed down for generations changed slightly. Different fears filled his imagination before we began, but the solution was the same as always. "Open your mouth," I said. "Learning is sweet."

Now we often sit together, working on schoolwork. Sometimes it's confusing trying to integrate two childrens' needs. Sometimes there is fear between us, and uncertainty. When those times appear, so does our jar of honey. The nicest part of this magick is that it works more than once.

Each day that we begin our learning together, each time we discover new things in the world around us, it connects us to our ancestors. When new skills are mastered, and confusion gives way to confidence, our family forms a Circle, and we say to each other, "Learning is sweet."

NEW SKILLS

Now that we have begun the process of formal education, whether we have chosen to educate at home, or have chosen public or private schools, the end result is ultimately the same. Somewhere in this transition, our children begin to acquire new skills at an almost alarming rate. One day we walk into a room and discover that our five-year-old can not only use the scissors, but has found out how to make snowflakes. Tools are more than interesting items, they are now useful ones, and just when did we stop having to pour that drink of milk for them? I can't remember exactly how it happened, but suddenly my services were no longer needed to prepare breakfast. Just when did it become safe to leave the house for a few minutes? Now, as never before, our refrigerators are art galleries, and we need to clean the fridge often to make way for science experiments.

We tend not to notice these new skills on a daily basis. It would probably be too scary if we did. Memories of postpartum set in. The baby once inside is now a child, fully and clearly her/his own person. We find that we are not needed in the same way as before. This is a time of bittersweet thoughts and feelings. Now we want to protect our children, and ourselves, from unwanted outside influences. We find ways to close ourselves off from things we remember as unpleasant experiences from our own childhoods. As our children ask more probing questions about the world around them, we find ourselves reaching for more rituals, more ways to express our viewpoints to them.

If we went to our family shrine and placed something there every time we noticed a new skill, a new point of independence, or gave thanks at a dinner for this new ability, we would be constantly reinforcing our children's self-esteem. When the scissors becomes a safe tool in their hands, a new pair of scissors, presented to them in a gift box at the family dinner table, has much more impact than would a compliment made in passing. Then, if we incorporate the skill into a ritual, or into a family act, we extend that feeling for our children. We need only to look at mythology and folk tales to find stories to highlight these skills.

"Mamma, where do the stars come from? And the snow-flakes? Do you know?"

"I have heard it in a story, little one. Listen now and hear how these things began.

'Once long and so long ago, the sky was empty at night. There were no stars to dance the dance and no Moon hung there to shine. The creatures that hunted the night gave prayers to the Earth Mother. They asked Her for a light to hunt by. But the creatures who hid in the night feared. They asked that the light of the night be soft, so they might be hidden by it.

The Earth Mother had an idea. She travelled deep into the Earth itself. There She found shining clusters of crystals. These She took with her to the surface. Carefully She worked to shape them. First She carved the Moon, and in her She placed a special blessing, that the Moon would change its face through all the month to remind us of when there was no Moon in the sky, and so that the hidden creatures could move freely once in the month. Then She carved out beautiful shining stars. These She gave a gift of dance, that if you gaze upon them long in the night sky they move about and seem to twinkle.

When She had carved them all, She climbed upon a great ladder and began to hang them one by one. She made beautiful shapes of hunters and hunted creatures. In this way She formed the great constellations. But the job was long and hard, and She grew weary. The Earth Mother climbed down from Her ladder to rest, and resting, slept.

Now, it happened that the old trickster, Coyote, came walking by, and he saw what the Earth Mother had been doing. He too wanted to make beautiful pictures in the sky. So up the ladder he climbed while the Mother slept. At first he tried to make pictures like the Mother had done, but he soon grew tired of the exacting work. So he took hold of the baskets of crystals, and threw them skyward, without thinking where they might fall, or find a place in the Mother's dance. Instead, he watched them blown by the wind, and cluster above wherever they blew.'

And that is why not all the stars are pictures, though some form shapes and patterns. And why the Milky Way is so very crowded with clusters of crystalline stars."

"But what about the snowflakes, Mommy?"

"The snowflakes come only in the winter, as you know. But do you know why? They are from the dust at the bottom of the baskets. The Earth Mother gave them each their own shapes, so that they would not be jealous of the stars. She wanted to be sure that when they fall, each one would be known for its own beauty, and order. When the Earth grows cold in the winter night, that tricky Coyote climbs to the sky to see if there are star pictures of Fire to warm him. But as he climbs, he clutches at the baskets the Mother used to carry the crystals skyward. As the baskets tip, a few fall out. And the Mother smiles, for Her children see the shapes of the snowflakes, and know the stars as She first dreamed them."

—adapted from a Native American Coyote tale.

KEYS

Of the many events that will occur in the early school years, acquiring keys to the house is one of the most important. Keys have long been associated with wisdom, responsibility, authority, independence and privacy. In ancient myths about Hecate, we find that the key is one of Her most treasured symbols. Today, many will place keys on shrines to Hecate to honor the Goddess of the Crossroads. In the Tarot, the Hierophant has two keys placed before him, representing the keys to knowledge. Diaries have locks and keys to guard their secrets. Heroes and celebrities are given the "keys to the city," a gesture of open house and welcome.

I have spoken with many adults about their experience with their first set of house keys. Often I am told of how they lost them, and got into trouble because of it. One young woman recounted a story of breaking into and entering her own home to avoid the anger her parents would express if they learned that she had lost her third set of keys. If only her younger brother had not fallen on the bathroom floor and required some dozen or so stitches, Mom might never have found out. Why did these keys get lost? In part, because children lose things. I asked these people if they felt that any real importance had been attached to the keys. Hardly any felt that they had. This seems strange. We give keys to our children, yet do we stress to them the trust involved in this? We allow them the run of our homes, trusting that they will continue to obey house and family rules, but we pass them the key to this trust without a word. Here, I believe, is the basis of all the lost keys.

When I was approaching the age when I was to be given house keys, I had long talks with my mother about the responsibility involved. There were hours spent discussing what to do in the event of an emergency, should one occur while I was at home alone after school. We discussed which friends could visit and which most certainly could not. And of course, we discussed how to unlock the door with my key and how to relock the door once I was inside.

The winter holidays arrived and there were many wonderful gifts to be opened. I remember that among my boxes there was one very small box with a bow on it. For some unknown reason, that was the box I opened first. Inside was a bright shiny new key to the house! It was the most beautiful thing I had ever seen. Not only did it mean that I was going to be allowed to let myself inside after school, it also meant that I would no longer have to go to a neighbor's house. This was confirmation that I was a big girl.

My mother went over the rules with me again the next day. She said that it was possible that she might be out when I got home that day, so I was to let myself in. School dragged that day and finally let out. Arriving home, with trembling hands I felt the locked door. My heart was pounding. I had never let myself into an empty house before. Slowly the key turned and even more slowly the door opened. But I heard a noise in the back of the apartment. Dare I go in? I listened and, disheartened, identified the sound of the shower. My mother was home. I was able to let myself in, but not to an empty house.

These rehearsals continued on and off for a few days. I would expect there to be no one at home, only to find someone napping or otherwise occupied. Doubts began to enter my mind. Was there never going to be a time when I would really be trusted? I had given up all hope. Then one day, I unlocked the door and walked inside. There was silence. "Sleeping," I thought. Quietly, I looked in the bedrooms. Empty. "Bathroom?" I wondered. Empty. It had happened. I was alone. Being like any other self-respecting child, I made a run for the kitchen. There on the table sat a vase with daisies in it and a note, which read: "Welcome home sweetheart. The cookies are in the blue bowl. Don't eat them all. Love, Mom" It is now more than twenty-five years later. I still have that key.

New skills and new responsibilities, perspectives change and transform almost daily. Listen to your five-year-old when speaking of a three-year-old child. Surely, without the benefit of school and new-found friends, this smaller child is only a baby. Nine-year-olds proudly announce that they have outgrown toys that were prized possessions only two months before. Questions about the world emerge. Demands are made about why things are. Harsh new vocabulary heralds the loss of innocence, and introduces the Age of Reason. "Why are people prejudiced?" "Do you think there will ever be an end to war?" "What's hell?"

As parents, we face one of the most difficult crossroads. Our answers will forever shape the way in which our children view the world around them. We must be cautious to respond honestly, and without malice. If we are asked about things for which we have no answer, then it is our job to look for one along with our children. Nowhere is this more important than in matters of spirituality. The conflicts and questions always come when we least expect them.

"Grandfather, is the lion really the mightiest of all the jungle animals?"

"Yes, that is true in all the stories I have heard the King of the Jungle tell. No matter which animal may

try to conquer the lion, he is the strongest, most wise
and the most courageous. So, yes, he is the mightiest of
all in the jungle."

"But Grandfather, in the stories about men in the
jungle man always wins. How can that be?"

"Who is tellingling the story little one?"

—adapted from an African Folktale.

When our daughter was six, in the last months of public
school and before we began to educate her at home, she was
troubled by a girl who had been her friend since preschool.
The girl had recently started Church school. She approached
our daughter several times, saying, "I can't play with you any
more, Maeghan. You're Pagan, you're going to go to Hell!"

Our daughter did not come to us right away. She has been
raised with pride in her religion, and pride in fighting her own
battles. We later learned that, after being confronted a
number of times, she finally turned to the girl and said, "I'd
rather go to Hell than have you tell me what religion to be!"

These are strong words for such a young child. Most adults
would never have been so blunt. Maeghan had determined
for herself that it was not worth fighting over this issue. The
question of "Hell" was moot for her, as well. Through careful
introduction to stories of other cultures and other world
religions, she was already grasping the idea that people are
different. None are better or worse than the others, they are
simply different.

This Age of Reason is not marked by a single ritual that
makes our children reasonable. Rather, it is a learning process
that goes on for several years. As the questions arise, each one
is addressed with respect and seriousness. During these early
years, while children still have the ability to see the magick in
the world around them, we must take the time to look at other
cultures and other religions with our children. I still remem-

ber the feeling of awe and almost jealousy when I visited a
Catholic mass with friends. The ritual drama was so very
different from my Jewish background, and the smells that
filled the Air left a lasting impression. How much more would
I have learned about the world if I also had been taken to a
Buddhist temple or Indian Pow-Wow? Would I have seen
more things in common than at odds?

Experience with children across the country who have
done that kind of early looking tells me that yes, the common
forms and repetitive thoughts are what make the deepest
impressions. Here is an opportunity to help the next generation to overcome forms of prejudice, and to work toward a
more solid understanding and respect for the other people
with whom we share this Earth.

And while we are sharing all of the major differences in
world religions, let's not leave out the differences within a
single path. It will do no good to raise children to see the
things in common between Christianity and Buddhists and
then have them come back unable to see that Wicca and the
Sioux share similar values.

Every religion teaches that the "Aquarian Age" or the
Messiah or some ideal state will occur if all people lead lives
based on their religion's good teachings. Try to make it a
practice to visit other rituals or read about them often in order
to help our children and ourselves to keep this in mind. By
sharing in this way, and by encouraging ourselves to follow all
the "good teachings," we may yet surprise each other with
how those far-off ideas can enter into everyday practice.

DEDICATION

Somewhere around the time that our children begin to lose
their teeth, they also expand their awareness of the world
around them. If they have been included in our rituals from

the beginning, they might well start to inquire about when they can take on a more active role. This is a sign that it is time to consider a dedication ritual for our children.

The Jiccaria Apache have a tale of a young girl who at age eight is given the gift of clay, a gift of the Earth Mother. Her grandmother retells the making of the first pipe and then marks the child's hands with clay. Now, relinked with her own grandmother's grandmothers, the girl fashions her first pipe out of clay. From now on she will be taught the mysteries of working clay, and her clay tools and figures will be used more and more by her family.

In agricultural societies, young girls began to help with the spinning and planting at this age. Young boys began to work in the fields. Working side by side with the adults, taking long walks with their grandparents and other elders, children were introduced to the mysteries that surrounded them everyday.

In our modern American culture, we find that children join clubs and organizations. A strong need to be formally involved in groups begins to develop as their views expand. In the modern Catholic Church, seven- and eight-year-olds are trained for First Communion. Why? Because at this point children are aware enough of what is going on around them on a spiritual level that they want to be included. They want to be grown-up.

Including our children in our rituals is a start. Allowing them to have a dedication ritual so that they feel more a part of the Circle is a way of expressing their importance to us, a way of expressing how welcome they are in our rituals, and a way of saying that the Gods are listening to them.

What exactly is a dedication? In this sense it refers to making a promise to be loyal to, to be actively involved with, this spiritual path. It in no way implies that your feelings will never change. Perhaps, in some traditions, it is also a statement of commitment to the Circle family. We must keep the child's point of view in mind for the dedication. Not having really lived long enough to make a comprehensive comparison of all their options, this is more a dedication to continued learning. The dedicant might decide to use a theme of continuing education, and promise to try to visit a different church or family each month. The theme might include some promise to the Earth Mother and Sky Father to help keep our home cleaner. Whatever the promise made, the rest of the Circle family must try to be as supportive as possible.

When our younger children have a Wiccaning Ritual, they are far too small to really play an active role. We are careful to ask only for guidance. Now with a child who has asked for a dedication, we must be careful to allow the promises and the focus of the ritual to be their's and not our own. This is not a place to play "spiritual one-up-manship." Take time to discuss what promises are and why they are important. Be extra cautious to remind both your child and yourself that a promise must come from a sincere desire to accomplish something, so that there must also be an element of practicality. Help them to focus on why they made their decision, and how to best carry it out.

When you have decided on the theme, you should write the ritual together. Discuss the order of the Circle, and which family members should have which parts. If there are other children in the family, explore the possibilities of giving them active roles. In some families this will be the first time that the child has had to create a ritual. As a resource person, your job is to guide the child and to check for continuity and practical elements. (Indoor Circles usually do not lend themselves to bonfires.)

We give more credibility to the Age of Reason when we demonstrate a willingness to help our children create their own ritual, and when we welcome them into the ritual family.

We gain respect and trust from our younger Circle members when we allow them to write the ritual for themselves. After the ritual is over, you might consider giving the new dedicant some special jobs related to the Circle. However you go about it, this is a time of great pride for all of the family to share.

4

PUBERTY RITES

Have you ever wondered at the depth of the ocean or the
height of the stars? Have you thought to count the leaves in
the forest or catch a ray of the Sun? Now as you take your
place in the dance of the World you will watch each turning
of the wheel with new eyes. Always remember your place in
this dance, as you begin to uncover its mystery.

—taken from a puberty riddle

One of the most important transitions in a person's life is the
onset of puberty. Yesterday a child, today a youth stands on
the threshold of adulthood. Their bodies are ignorant of
cultural restrictions and restraints; urges take over. Hor-
monal messages send emotions on roller coaster rides, leaving
confusion and, all too often, fear in their wake.

The rituals of Holding Hands with the Sun and Holding
Hands with the Moon, are ways to help cross the threshold of
adulthood. By giving ritual significance to these biological
events we give honor to those changes and pave the way for
future growth within our communities. Although both
rituals are timed to coincide with puberty's onset, they are not
mirror images of each other. The manner in which we
introduce the beginning of sexual awareness is also not to be
underplayed. If we can take a few extra moments to try to
convey the idea of caring and responsible sexuality, then we
further assist the next generation to overcome many handi-
caps left to us and to our parents. By demonstrating a

conscious link between our body's cycles and the cycles of the Goddess and God we once again bring the sacred into everyday life.

Two stories adapted from British folklore and custom are offered to help incorporate some of these ideas. The stories will further enhance the idea that while both rituals are indeed very different in their nature, their purposes are ultimately intertwined.

HOLDING HANDS WITH THE SUN

A young man walked with his companions over the calm English countryside. Snow lay over the fields and pine groves, muffling the sound of the boys' footsteps and animated talk. Today was special for all of them, but especially for this young man.

Tonight all of them would go together to hunt the Wren, for tomorrow would be Yule, the Winter Solstice. The Wren is the King of Winter, and to celebrate the return of the Sun, a wren would be hunted, and his body taken from door to door so that all could share in the joy of this token of the death of winter. Yule, the longest night of the year. The death of the Wren, and the laughter of the boys, were symbols of the promise that the Sun would be reborn, and would grow with the new season.

But today was this young man's day. It was the day of cutting the Yule tree.

He had seen the other boys each year, the boys who had come into their Suntime. Each year a boy who had come closer to the God in this way earned the honor of choosing a tree. It was hard to choose, for many trees had been planted over the graves of the mothers and fathers who had gone before. Groves held whole families beneath them, and indeed, when this boy died, he hoped to be buried in his family's grove, with a tall pine or a strong oak over him. And if he had hunted well, or had in some other way honored the God, perhaps he would lie beneath an alder or a rowan. His own grandfather lay in the rowan grove, for he had led the hunters each fall to the meadow where the largest herds grazed. Grandfather was strong with the Hunting Magick.

Now the boy's time was here. Hair had grown on his body, and seed was within him. When spring came, he could draw the God down to him, and honor the Goddess at the Maypole, as he had seen the young folks do each year. As a young boy he had laughed, and wondered how those couples could run naked to the Maypole field, and caress like that in the still summer evening. But now it didn't seem silly or unimportant. Now the girls he had grown up with looked soft and beautiful to him, and he shook a little when he thought that he would share with them the rite of the Maypole.

But that would be in the spring. First, the Yule tree must be chosen and cut, and he had come into his Suntime. It was he who would choose the tree.

The boys came into the older pine grove. The group quieted now. Each of them had stood there before, under the grey winter sky, knowing that his decision would influence the crop and the babes born this year. They stood, looked at the young man, and waited.

He looked around. These were the Grandfather trees. Here were buried the old ones who had gone long before. Some had lived so long ago that the Fair ones, the Fairies, had spoken to them while they were alive. This was before the Normans came, and the Fair ones went north to the wild places. Here were buried his grandfather's grandfathers. Oh, how would he choose?

But he remembered his grandfather, in whom the Hunting magick had run strong. He raised his arms to the grey winter sky.

"Come to me, Grandfather," he whispered. "Help me choose."

Suddenly there was a flutter in the forest. A wren, the King of Winter, flew by. It swept over the young man's head, and then lit on a nearby tree, singing. The wren, whom the Fair ones called Cutty Vran, Bran's sparrow. The bird of Bran, the Winter King. The bird looked at the young man, and flew off. The young man smiled.

"Thank you, Grandpa," he whispered. "We cut this one," the young man told his companions. The other boys stood still, quiet.

"Why do you stand there?" the young man asked, anxious. "Have I not chosen?"

Finally one of his companions spoke, an older one who had honored the Goddess at the Maypole for several springs, and hoped to marry this June.

"You have chosen," he said. "We'll cut this down in no time."

Then, more quietly, he echoed the thought of each there.

"The magick is strong in you," he said.

Long gone are the days of the elders taking our sons off to their vision quests. Nor do we often suggest that they go out and hunt the sacred deer. Here, in modern America, we hear horror stories of young boys being taken to the "other side of town," sent in to a strange woman who will "initiate" him.

There was a time when coming into puberty for a boy

meant becoming a man in a tangible sense. Ritual challenges to test his strength, hunting skills, battle skills and wisdom all joined together to help him accept this new role in his society. These skills were all a major part of contributing to his community, not just arbitrary tests to prove manliness. We have no real corollary to these tests. Should we send our young men off to the supermarket with limited funds to shop for a week as a simulation of the hunt? Would travelling through the inner city's rush hours demonstrate battle skills?

More practical options would be to take our sons and have them demonstrate camping and hunting skills, or do ritual drumming. But I think of those of us from the city, where these are alien skills. No, there is a need to do something more than earn a Boy Scout merit badge. The old rituals proved that boys were contributors to the community, not merely tough.

Holding Hands with the Sun must point to the options available to our sons. We need to bridge childhood and adulthood without being lured into a side trip into areas unrelated. New sexual urges need to be recognized, but not aggrandized. If we can find ways to welcome our sons into the adult world without asking them to carry our baggage, then we set the tone for a whole generation of caring, strong men. Here we must focus on the image of the loving, caring God, not the all-knowing, controlling God so many of us have rebelled against.

Choosing the Guides

The participants in this ritual will all be men. Men from the Circle will represent a Godfather (mentor) and five roles important in men's lives. The choices should be based upon who most strongly feels the part, not necessarily on the ages of the participant. The Godfather should, however, be chosen with extra care. He will become a mentor for the son and will as form a magickal bond with the family. The roles are:

Godfather: Should the family be fortunate enough to have remained close to the Godfather who was present for the Wiccaning, he might be a logical choice to portray the Godfather here. Whoever accepts this role needs to have a close relationship with the son and with the father. He should be someone whom the son admires or who has been able to assist the boy in decision making.

Youth: Another man portrays the Youth. This figure represents all of the primal urges and questions from earliest childhood. This guide will stand as a reminder that even though we leave behind our childhood, the child within never dies. He also represents unlimited potential.

Dreamer: As the world opens for our sons, we want to remember the dreams that help to shape the choices that we make. The Dreamer guide remembers every wish, hope and fear that each of us has. He offers the world to those who have the courage and the faith to reach out for it.

Father: Every male has an instinct to protect, shield and nurture. The Father offers us advice and wisdom. His job is to find the lessons in all things and to share our wonder of the world around us. It is also he who will teach us the beauty of unconditional love. This Father is not the same person as the the father of the boy undergoing this ritual.

Grandfather: Time grants us the gift of reflection, and it is our Grandfathers who remember the stories. Here is the culmination of a life's work, and the grandeur of wisdom. Our Grandfather guide also tells us that even though we grow old, we are still a child.

Priest: As we seek to define our spiritual selves, the Priest guides us to that higher being. The Priest is the embodiment of all qualities that reflect the God in everyday life.

The Priest will annoint the son with oil as part of this ritual. Have ready an oil made from 1 part patchouli oil, 1/2 part vetivert oil, 1/2 part dark musk oil, a few drops each of orange (neroli) oil and cinnamon oil. Blend all the oils together and perhaps add to a neutral oil base such as apricot.

The Ritual

The area chosen for the ritual should be prepared early in the day. If there has been a decision to hold an all-night vigil beforehand, then you might prepare the site during the night. The ritual should be held during the daylight hours. All invited guests should bring something that symbolizes themselves. You may have a teacher who brings a book, or a carpenter who brings tools. Other symbols might include cooking tools, instruments, dolls, art supplies, beepers or ritual tools. The purpose is to demonstrate options for men in our society. The son should also bring something that symbolizes his own childhood.

The son should spend much of the day (or the night before) with his Godfather, while his father is given a chance to reflect by himself. Since the ritual will forever change the way in which father and son look at each other, they are encouraged to spend the day apart from one another, allowing them each personal space in which to prepare for the ritual.

The guides are stationed either along a path to the Circle or around the Circle itself. The Father is standing as part of the Circle. Various members of the group should be given the role of casting the Circle. While creating the space, call on the qualities that reflect the mood of the Circle. In the East you might ask for childhood wonder and growing intelligence. The South might reflect finding true will, the West freedom to show emotion without fear. The North might be asked to bring the gift of constancy and manifestation. Inviting the God and Goddess places balance inside the Circle, and helps to keep us focused on being part of a greater family.

The son may take some time to meditate before beginning. He will have his symbol of childhood with him. When he is ready, he walks to his Godfather.

Godfather: *(Taking the childhood symbol.)* Today you prepare to enter the larger family of the brotherhood of men. Though you are no longer the little boy of yesterday, do not be fooled into believing that you are no longer a child. We are children of the God and Goddess. You are merely walking through one of the many doorways of your life, and allowing yourself to become a fuller, richer person. This symbol of your childhood is changing as you redefine yourself and accept more responsibility within our community.

They walk together toward the Youth.

Youth: Welcome brother. I am Youth, I am the potential of all young men. It has been my voice and my urging that has driven you, even as a baby. I was there to guide your first steps. Through my eyes you gazed upon the stars and wondered why they shone. When the wind sang to you, I helped you to understand the words. As you grew and formed friendships, I was there with you to help you see beyond your own self. My questions became yours as you learned to interpret the expanding world around you.

When those around you said that you could not do something that your heart said was possible, I helped you to block out their negative thoughts and to find the strength to go on and to prove to yourself that all things were possible. Each task, each test, I met with the same energy. Whether it was learning to climb the monkey-bars, nurturing your pets and those around you, or mastering the skills of reading and writing, I gave you the self-confidence to try to succeed.

Now you have grown into a young man. Your body is no longer the body of a small boy, your mind begins to probe deeper questions and to ask more of the world. The temper tantrums of early childhood must give way to reason and debate. You do not leave me behind as you grow. As the challenges grow more complex, as you have need to unravel things for yourself, I will still be there to guide and to encourage you. Even when you have grown old, I will still be seen as the twinkle in your eyes and the laughter of your heart. Never letting the wonderment of the little boy inside you be destroyed, together we will grow.

Accept this gift of your youth. It is a symbol of your unlimited potential. *(He gives the son a small pouch or bag, which is empty.)*

Son and Godfather walk to the Dreamer.

Dreamer: I am the Dreamer. You have come to me by way of your dreams and hopes. All the things that you have ever wanted and sought in your life are part of me. Each of us has a piece of the stars, a spark of the Gods, locked deep inside. Your youthfulness has given you motivation, but my dreams are what makes the effort worthwhile. Though you may not know it, you are at my doorway and are about to enter my world.

Worlds that have only been a fantasy become reality when you find the way inside. As a baby, you dreamed the dream of love. You found this in the arms of your mother and father. Time passed and you wondered if you would find a love of your own. Once you have crossed my threshold, the journey will begin. But my dreams are not only made of love. Each time you wished, each time you reached for the stars, I was there beside you to guide your hand. And when you dreamed dreams that brought fear to you, and you cried, it was my tears that ran down your cheeks.

Remember me every time you have the opportunity to make a choice. These choices come to you at the bidding of your dreams. If you wish it, the Moon and the stars are yours for the taking. Nothing good in the world is beyond your grasp. This tonka bean is a gift from me. It is for making wishes become real. Place it inside your pouch and fill your own potential with your wishes. (*He gives son the tonka bean.*)

The Godfather takes the son to the Father Guide.

Father: Every little boy has a Father. Life would not be possible without the first gift of his seed. That is only the beginning. To be a real father, you must learn to love and protect. I am that part of you, the part that has always sought to find the good in all those around you. Even when you have experienced the harshness that the world can sometimes offer, it was I who tried to teach you to look beyond. When you, or those you loved were threatened by others, I gave you the caring to try to protect them.

You must learn to find love around you in order to be able to give the gift of life. When the time is right for you, I will be at your side to teach that love is not just for a moment, but is a lasting commitment, to be cherished and nurtured. And when those you love must move beyond or away, I will also be there to show you that love can be transformed as well as transform those it touches.

You have watched me and learned from me with each turning of the wheel. I can be seen in the growing and harvesting of the grains.

My lessons are simple, and you have been hearing them your whole life. For it was my presence that you felt when your heart filled with warmth for those around you as you learned to love. I was there when you first cried out in pain, and needed to be heard. I helped you learn that to care for those around you, sometimes meant that you had to say "no".

Now as you become a man in our Circle, I will stay at your side to help you find yourself. I offer you unconditional love and, as you gain self-confidence, I will teach you to offer this gift to those people who are special in your world. For now, I give you a small mirror. Keep this in your pouch to remind you that all your wishes and dreams are nothing without first loving yourself. *(He gives the mirror.)*

Son and Godfather walk to the Grandfather.

Grandfather: I am your Grandfather. My life has been full and rich, though not without its tears. When I was younger, old age seemed far away, something that could never happen to me. Now, you might think that my youth seems far off. This is not true. I am the totality of all of my experiences. All that I had wished for, worked for and fought for in my life is now a part of me. The lines on my face, the gray in my hair are all part of my story. No longer do I have to work as I once did. The

Sunrises and Sunsets are there for me to enjoy. I can watch the passing of the seasons without fear. For I have learned that there will always be another turning of the wheel.

Perhaps you think that I have not also been a part of you. This also is not true. Even during your experiences as a young child, I whispered wisdom in your ears and guided you through your earliest trials. I helped you to make all of your hardest decisions. When you had need to separate yourself from others, or to give away those things that were dear to you, I stood by you to make the separations easier.

Now is the time of your very first sowing. From tonight on you will be more responsible for who you choose to become. If you'd like, I will tell you all the old stories. You have only to listen with your heart. The wisdom that you may believe I have is already deep inside of you. I give you these seeds, to place inside your pouch. Keep them always, to remember that the things you reap will be the same things that you planted. *(He gives his gift of seeds.)* Always remember that simple rule, and your life will be all the richer.

They now walk toward the Priest.

Priest: Welcome. You have now seen your own potential unfold before you. I am the Priest that is a part of all men. My presence has been with you from the very beginning. Each time you listened to those people who needed a friend, I was with you. I gave you the confidence to seek your higher self, even when you were urged by others to ignore my voice.

I am the most elusive part of yourself. Though you could find me if you searched long enough and hard enough, I am most easily found by looking at others. It is true that the God can be found in any man, but only those who are willing to look beyond the everyday will find the gentle God, who is so sure of himself that He has no need to prove himself. I stand here now to show you that this is possible for you, as well. If you would look at the world as I see it, then you will be able to find the spark of the divine in all things around you.

Now you have begun to fill your pouch with gifts. I give you the gift of an anointing to herald your new place in our Circle. You may choose to repeat each line after me.

The Priest anoints each part of the son as he speaks these lines.

(*Anointing his head.*) Bless me God of the Green Places, for I am your son.

(*Anointing his Third Eye, or the center of his forehead.*) Bless my mind that it may always grow and explore the world around me.

(Anointing his mouth.) Bless my lips that they speak only with truth, love and honor.

(Anointing his heart.) Bless my heart that it is always filled with compassion and courage.

(Anointing his genitals.) Bless my seed that it be a gift of life given in true love.

(Anointing his knees.) Bless my knees that I may always know the lessons of humility.

(Anointing his feet) Bless my feet that I may walk with an inner confidence on the path I choose.

(Anointing his hands.) Bless my hands that they may bring caring, creativity and protection to all around me.

(Anointing his head once again.) And bless me God of the Green Places, for I am your son.

This oil is yours to keep. Its scent is the scent of new promise and strength. Use it whenever you feel the need to recall this moment. Go now and face your father, he is waiting. *(He turns the son to face his father.)*

During the anointing the Godfather has joined the others in the Circle.

Godfather: *(Stepping in front of the son.)* Wait, there is still one gift that you must receive before you

face your father again. You have been shown
your potential, but not yet shown your
choices. Before you lay many paths. In time
you may choose to walk yet a different path.
All of us who have gathered here are only a
portion of a still larger brotherhood. Our
paths, though varied, may never become
yours. Listen to those who love you, and hear
not only the choices that they have made, but
also hear the courage that it has taken for each
to choose for himself.

Each member of the Circle now comes forward, picks up his
own symbol and states who he is. The father remains silent.

Godfather: You have now been given almost all of the
                choices that we represent. *(Bringing forward
                the son's childhood symbol.)* You also may
                choose to keep this part of you as you grow.
                (Returning the symbol to the son.) Growing
                older does not have to mean giving away your
                childhood.

                Finally, there is a gift from me. There will be
                times when you need to speak to someone
                older who has had the benefit of experience.
                I promise that I will there to listen, and not to
                judge. For those times when you would
                speak to your father, but cannot, I will give
                you my time and caring. Also, I have this gift
                for you to add to your pouch. *(He gives him
                a small gift of his own choosing.)* Now you
                must go back to your father, no longer as a
                little boy but as a young man.

The son goes to his father.

Father: Welcome. Tonight you are no longer just my
               son, you are also my brother. I have watched
               you grow and I have rejoiced in each triumph.
               When you cried I, too, felt tears in my eyes,
               and your laughter has brought happiness to
               me. Now you approach a time of your own.
               Your body must now learn to respond to its
               own inner rhythms and we must both learn to
               listen to each other.

               When you were very small, I was the giant
               who could do the impossible for you. Now,
               through the eyes of a young adult, you can
               see that I am only a man. I have had to learn
               to let you go and find yourself. Every year has
               changed our relationship and reshaped our
               worlds. If this were another time, you would
               leave my world and find your own way. But
               that is not the case today. Perhaps I am selfish
               when I tell you I am glad that you will not
               leave my house just yet. There are many new
               mysteries and adventures for us to explore
               together. I am looking forward to sharing all
               of those with you.

               Today, let all who have gathered here with us
               know that you are now free to make more
               decisions for yourself and are to be counted
               on to carry out more responsibility within our
               family. Now you are a part of the larger
               brotherhood that has always bound men
               together. We are all proud of you, but none
               so much as myself. *(He gives his son a gift.)*

Now is time for sharing stories and other gift-giving. If your Circle dances or drums, you might allow the son to lead. If you usually work in a mixed male/female Circle, you might now invite the women in to share Wine and Cakes, again allowing the Son to do the blessing.

When the time is correct, close the Circle and spend the day outdoors, continuing to celebrate the new bonds that were forged during the ritual.

HOLDING HANDS WITH THE MOON

"Keep your mind on your sewing, girl."

Her aunt's words were quick, but she knew auntie wasn't angry. She turned her eyes away from the window, back to the Sunlit cottage room that smelled of berries and drying heather.

"Aye, he's a fine lad," her auntie said, smiling and nodding her grey head out toward the field where the young men practiced the Morris dancing. The young woman, surprised, blushed and lowered her head.

"And they say," her auntie whispered, "that the magick is strong in him."

"Do you think it's so?" the younger one asked, too interested now to cling to her modesty.

"Do I think it's so? Oh, girl, you're no fool. Look at him dancing. You can see it, or you're blind."

The young woman felt her cheeks redden, and turned back to sewing. She had come to her Moon time as the Yule turned. The shredded slip before her was the slip she'd been wearing when her first blood flowed. Her mother had held it aside, carefully folding in the dried brown blood of life that stained it. Now, the Yule was past. The fields were warm, and the people danced again, the men in bells in the sunny fields, the young women laughing and shrieking as they leaped the Fire, clad in dew and starry night.

Now was the time to take her blood-stained slip and sew it, as the other young women would do, into ribbons for the Maypole.

The Maypole stood already in the field where the young men danced. At Yule it had been the pine tree, decked in candles and red ribbons. At Candlemas, the branches had been stripped and used to kindle the Balefires. Now, branchless, the Grandfather tree stood in the field, ready, waiting. Tomorrow those young men would dance the May, winding around the pole the ribbons that were once slips worn by girls young and lean, who had looked up at the stars and wondered aloud to the Moon when their breasts would grow and their bodies change with the mark of the Mother. Girls who had wakened one day to discover breasts and soft pubic hair. Girls who were now women, and who now danced the Fire. Young women who would honor the Mother at the Maypole. The Maypole, where her own slip would be a ribbon, sewn by her hands in the Sunlit cottage of her auntie, woven by the boys into a web that spoke of the secrets of the Mother.

"Has he noticed you?" her aunt asked.

"I think so," she said. She'd seen him watching her, and she'd cursed the youthfulness that tied her tongue. She never realized he'd also felt anger at himself for being young and unsure of himself. "At the Maypole," he'd told himself, burning. "At the Maypole," she'd whispered as she watched him in his Morris bells and ribbons.

"Aye, I've seen him glance at you," her auntie chuckled. "As all the boys have. You're a beauty."

Beltane morning came in Sunlight and laughter. The

girls had run naked through the fields, then dressed to watch the boys play tug of war and badger in the bag. A few of the girls even played this year. Strength was something the people prized in either gender.

Finally the fiddler started playing Hallentow. All the people, young and old, ran to the field for the dance. He caught her eye as he wove the ribbon in and out among the ribbons of the other young men. He heard her laughter weave above the fiddle music and the noise of the old ones clapping and shouting praise to the dancers. Each knew the magick there.

Her eyes widened as she saw the ribbon in his hand, the ribbon she had sewn.

He had taken hold of her ribbon, pretending to joke as he pushed the other boys out of the way. But they knew, or had been told by their elders. The magick was strong in him. And in her. When she sang the milking songs, the milk never soured. When it was she who told the old stories, all listened. And when she danced the Fire, and leaped, her new-grown breasts pale and soft in the moonlight, the women felt it. The Mother spoke through this shy, beautiful woman-child. When she bore, each farmer would beg her to walk skyclad through his field, singing the songs of ripening the Fair Ones had taught them, and spilling her milk on the furrows.

He danced the Maypole, never knowing the things the elders said about them, and hoping that she'd notice that he held her ribbon.

Night was starry, the Moon a thin, waxing crescent. He lay beside her, feeling her sighing, hearing the excited breathing of the other young couples. He'd felt the magick in her, and she in him. As he gave his seed to her, she'd felt the breath of Mab, the Mother. She'd heard a strange voice, a whisper, that had taught her Mab's true name. She was sure the Horned One had spoken to him in the same way.

He kissed her. She held his head to her breast, and whispered the True Name of the Mother to the stars.

A young girl celebrates her entrance into young womanhood at the full Moon following her first blood. In older cultures this rite would have marked a woman's readiness to bear children. In our culture this is often an awkward limbo between childhood and adulthood. A once familiar image in the mirror has blossomed and grown shapely. The body's natural urges are making themselves felt but society says that it is not yet time to act on them.

We give our girls a different message than the one they may, regrettably, get in school or from friends whose lifeway differs from ours. As our girls reach this strange and wonderful time, we take pleasure in sharing and celebrating with them. All women and girls are invited to this ritual. The rite of a girl coming into her puberty gives our adults a way to celebrate what they may not have had at the same time in their own lives, and it shows our children that each transition has its own beauty.

The ritual site is prepared ahead of time. A Circle is cast to include as much space as possible. Each guide will be stationed either outside the Circle, if space allows, or at the quarter points.

It is very important that the mother and daughter are separated as early in the ritual preparations as possible. The daughter should spend the day with her Goddessmother. The mother should spend the day with friends and should be pampered and shown special treatment. Both the mother and the daughter should be encouraged to talk about feelings, and should be given foods that make them feel good.

As with the ritual for sons, daughters are anointed. A daughter's anointing oil may be made from 1 part carnation oil, 1/2 part lotus oil, 1/2 part jasmine oil, blended into a light musk base, or other light scented base oil. Add a few sprigs of lemon balm to the oil.

The daughter should also be given a ritual bath. For her bath, add a few drops of the oil to the Water. You might also add white rose petals and daisies to float in the tub, and few spoonfuls of sea salt.

Choosing the Guides

This ritual is done by a Circle of women. Women will play roles representing female experince. They are:

Goddessmother: An adult who is close to both the mother and the daughter should be chosen as Goddessmother. If the same woman who was present for the Wiccaning is still involved with the family, she would be an excellent choice. Unlike the other guides, she will be making a very real and magickal bond with both the mother and the daughter.

Maiden: The Maiden should be a woman who is perhaps not much older that the daughter, but who has become sexually aware (though not necessarily active). She will represent the transition from young girl to young woman.

Mother: The Mother should be a woman who has already borne children and raised them for several years. She should be someone who, to mother and daughter, represents the mother within all women.

Crone: We are all richer when we are blessed with the presence of those who have lived and gained wisdom from their lives.

Representing the fruits of a lifetime, the Crone reminds the daughter that what she sows now lays the real foundation for what she will reap in her life.

Priestess: If all women are, in some way, a reflection of the divine presence of the Goddess, the Priestess helps us to remember this. In her, we find our way to the higher self.

The Ritual

The ritual site has been prepared. The casting of the Circle should be centered on the feelings of change. Invite the Quarters to bring aspects reflecting the four elements of womanhood (Maiden, Mother, Crone, Priestess). Inviting both Goddess and God maintains a balance, reminding us that we are always children of the Universe. The guides are standing in the Quarters or, if space permits, they may be stationed along a path to the ritual site. The daughter is given a ritual bath by the young women to help prepare her, and she is dressed in a white robe. Her Goddessmother accompanies her to the Circle. As they walk they may talk about their feelings, or the excitement of the ritual ahead. They are first met by the Maiden.

Maiden: I am the little girl that lives on in all women. I am the child who plays and wonders. In all things I find beauty and magick. I stood by your side when you were small and nurtured your dolls and pets. When your mother needed to be mothered, I too was there, learning the gentle arts of loving and caring. When you were treated cruelly by your friends and learned to return that cruelty, it was I who flushed red in your cheeks and let your tears flow. As you grew, and your body seemed to betray you, changing without your bidding, I was there to help you find peace within yourself and to celebrate your growth.

I will hold your hand and stay by your side as you face this wonderful threshold of change and transition, as you once held onto your dolls' hands to comfort them through fears. I will help you to learn and explore new mysteries as you grow confident with your new self. Together we will find beauty and magick in a changing world. When the time is right, I will help you open the doorway to your own deep mysteries, and find the secrets of love.

But remember this: no matter where your path may take you, no matter how long your lifetime, there will always be a small child filled with wonder, living inside of you.

Accept this token to remember me by. *(She gives the daughter a white rose.)*

Daughter and Goddessmother proceed to the Mother.

Mother: In all women there lives a mother. She may appear to some as warm, gentle and nurturing, to others strong and fiercely independent. But she lives on in all women, and in me. Some will tell you that you now stand at my doorway. I tell you that you have always stood with me. It was my hand that guided yours when you responded to the calls of need around you. I helped you place each

seed as you learned to plant in your garden.
It was I who reminded you to Water and feed
them. When you taught your pets the rules of
your world, I lent you the strength to yell at
those you loved, and courage to comfort their
cries.

As your awareness of the world expands and
your experiences grow, it is I who will comfort the little girl still inside. Though your
body cries out to embrace my mysteries, it is
my love that will help you learn the right
time. My lessons are full and wonderful. In
your time, I will guide you into worlds that
are only fantasies now. It will be I who aids
you as you leave your cherished dolls behind
to embrace others fully in love, and if you
wish, to bear a child. But these are for later,
now I will be your friend and ally in a strange
and exciting world. Listen to my voice when
you are unsure of yourself, and there you will
find new depth and insight. Ask for my hand
when you feel alone and afraid, and you will
find unconditional love. I offer you strength
and will, purpose and stability. Though at
times I may appear harsh and unbending, you
will someday come to understand that all the
love and wonder I offer is not given without
first accepting responsibility.

I offer you this red rose as a token. It is a
flower of fullness and of deep and true love.
Accept it, and accept that part of you is part of
me. *(She gives the daughter a red rose.)*

Daughter and Goddessmother now proceed to the Crone.

Crone: All cycles have beginnings and endings. Now
        you are at the beginning of a real and true
        mystery. From where you stand, I must seem
        foreign and very far away. Yet I have never
        left your side. It was I, the Crone, who stood
        by you when you ruthlessly decided which
        dolls were to be sent away, or which puppies
        and kittens could not live in your house. As
        you learned each lesson of selection and
        separation, it was my inner wisdom that
        guided you and gave you courage to face the
        next.

        Now life is full for you. Your blood flows
        freely with the changing of the Moon. Later,
        when your cycle has slowed and your blood
        flow has dried, I will be there to guide you
        back through the same door you now step
        through. Though my blood has ceased to
        flow, my life is full and rich. I have learned
        with each passing cycle, and have grown from
        the experience. Many will tell stories of pain,
        anger and confusion. You will often hear of
        those who lose control of their lives from the
        blood. If you have the courage to call on me,
        my arms will hold you and give you renewed
        strength. I will help to teach you that each
        cycle has its own ending, and seeing through
        my eyes, you will find less fear.

        Remember, as you stand now at the begin-
        ning, that all beginnings offer choices. You

may choose to see the beauty of your own cycle, or you may choose to find it a burden. Accept these ferns. Some see them as a thing of beauty. But they are a deadly poison if used incorrectly. May they serve to remind you that you now have the choice to see all things in their beauty or in their darkness. When you have planted, may your harvest be bountiful. *(She gives the daughter the ferns.)*

Daughter and Goddessmother walk to the Priestess.

Priestess: Welcome. You have been brought to this portal by those who love you. Love is the spark of the divine. I am the divine that is in all women. We all strive to find that part of ourselves that can reach beyond the stars. Though I have always been a part of you, it is not so easy for you to find me on your own. I am that part of you that has always offered love and caring, even when your own heart was breaking. It was through my eyes that you sought the good in everything, even when others would ask you to see the darkness that their eyes saw. As you continue to grow, I will be with you to help you look outside of yourself, for the divine that you see in me exists in all the world around you.

My sisters have given you gifts to know them by. I offer you the anointing of womanhood. You may repeat each line after me if you choose.

The Priestess anoints each part of the daughter's body as the lines are spoken.

(Anointing her head.) Bless me Goddess for I am your daughter.

(Anointing her Third Eye.) Bless my mind that it be open to learn Your mysteries.

(Anointing her mouth.) Bless my lips that they will speak in love and wisdom.

(Anointing her breasts.) Bless my breasts that grow full in beauty.

(Anointing her womb.) Bless my womb that reveals the mysteries of the cycles of life, death and rebirth.

(Anointing her knees.) Bless my knees that will kneel to teach me humility.

(Anointing her feet.) Bless my feet, which have brought me here and help them to walk with confidence and purpose.

(Anointing her hands.) Bless my hands that they may be used to create beauty in this world.

(Anointing her head again.) And bless me Goddess, for I am Your daughter.

Now I offer you this oil. It is the smell of

beauty, and the oil that tokens your womanhood. Use it when you feel the need. Go
now, your mother waits for you. *(She gives the
daughter the oil and points her toward the
center, where her mother is standing.)*

During the anointing, the Goddessmother has left the
daughter's side. When she sees the daughter begin to walk
towards her mother, she steps between the two.

Goddessmother: Wait. You still walk toward your mother
with the steps of a child. Tonight you have
moved beyond the child and have begun
the transformation into a woman. You
approach the mother who gave you life,
but from this night your life is truly your
own. I have held your hand through your
childhood. I have watched you grow, and
have waited until this day. Now I have a
promise that I wish to make.

Your first blood is like the seed of the
flowers that you have been given. It marks
a time of growth and change. Not the
growth of the little girl you were, but the
growth into the woman you are becoming.
During the next few years you will need to
learn new skills, to accept yourself and to
discover yourself in new ways. There may
come a time when you need a mother's
counsel, but cannot speak to the mother
who birthed you. I promise to be there to
assist you. I promise to listen, and to
counsel you in those times. I am your

mother in the Goddess. I will always be
with you, as a friend and as a sister. *(She
gives the daughter a gift of her choosing.)*

Now the daughter faces her Mother.

Mother: Tonight I welcome you not just as my child,
             but also as my sister. I have nurtured you,
             and loved you as you have grown. Each year
             has brought us closer to each other, and
             through your eyes I have seen many myster-
             ies. Now we share a bond that echoes from
             our beginnings. From this night on you are
             also bound to all women from the beginning
             of time, just as I was bound in my time, and
             my mother in her's. All of us gathered here
             tonight have come to see our divine selves in
             that bond that we now celebrate with you.

             In days long ago, it would have been time to
             release you from my house. You would have
             chosen you own place as a fully accepted,
             adult woman. But times have changed and,
             perhaps selfishly, I am glad of it. Now you are
             free to make more decisions for yourself and
             to find more freedoms, but I will be able to
             share those joys with you. Together we can
             explore and grow. When you were very little
             I could be your entire world. As you learned
             to walk and to find your independence, I
             learned to let go of some of that control.
             Now you respond to an inner rhythm that is
             beyond both of us. We must both learn to
             respect that, and each other.

As we hold hands under the first Moon of
your womanhood, I give you a gift that will
always bring you back to this night. Welcome
daughter, sister, friend. *(She gives her daughter a piece of jewelry with a red stone.)*

All the women gathered are now invited to speak to the
daughter and share stories, food and drink. If the group feels
moved to dance a spiral dance, have the daughter lead.

For those Circles that usually work with both men and
women, it is time to invite the men into the Circle. Have the
daughter bless the Wine and Cakes with a male member of the
Circle.

Close the Circle when it feels right to do so.

The completion of the Puberty Rites marks the beginning of
young adulthood. There was a time when our children would
have left our homes at this point to make a place for themselves in the larger world. In our society that is not the case.
How we incorporate these changes in our teens will have a
very lasting effect on the rest of our family's relationships.
Having acknowledged in a public ritual that adulthood has
begun, we must make the adjustments to allow for increased
input as well as for increased responsibility.

It would be impossible to look at either our children or
ourselves and ignore the sudden interest in sex. We must find
a way to demonstrate our trust at this time, and we must
emphasize the need to be responsible about the sexual choices
made. If we have raised our children in a truly open and caring
environment, then we have little to worry about, the lines of
communication will already exist and we must work to keep
them open and honest. This is a time of linking the child to
the adult worlds. Our job is to help them to assume responsibility easily, without robbing our children of the experiences
themselves.

For some, this will mark the beginning of a rebellion. As we know, all young adults must test their new-found freedoms and it usually comes as some sort of rebellion within the family. Allow these rituals to soothe over some of the possible hurt. Rely on your extended family to help keep your mind focused on growth, not tearing down everything you have worked to build. If your teen suddenly changes the direction of his/her spiritual path, and many will, try to remember that most of us found our paths by looking beyond what our families offered us. Having given your child a positive spiritual experience filled with respect, she/he will find the path that is best for him/her and will always have the magick with which you filled his/her childhood.

When we celebrate the Age of Reason, we set the stage for a lifetime of reasonable solutions to possible conflicts and wonderful sharing within our family. Now, we must move forward and begin to put the magick of our rites into action by assuming more responsibility within the greater world.

5

ASSUMING RESPONSIBILITY

You have been given the gift of freedom. Would you use
your gift to enslave the world around you? Having freedom,
you must learn to use wisdom to moderate your choices.
Only with carefully measured responsibility will you become
the person of your dreams. There is no magick that can alter
the nature of the world. Working within its equilibrium you
will find all things possible.

—from a traditional meditation

We spend the majority of our lives as adults. Although we are
always faced with choices to be made and decisions to be
considered, as adults the stakes are higher. There was a time
when the impact of adulthood was felt immediately upon
reaching puberty. Now there is a transition period. During
the first few years, many young adults will experience their
first sexual union, move out of their parents' homes, get cars
and telephones, and find jobs. Even with all of these adult
trappings, however, they will not be considered to be adults.
Our society has set that on a calendar, and we must be patient
during these intervening years.

After this great emancipation has occurred, we are counted
on to accept more and more responsibility. The questions
that demand our attention become more complex. So much
energy is spent on simply trying to live in our world that it
becomes easy to forget the magick around us. We need to find
ways to re-connect ourselves. In the rush to survive the

artificial restraints of a modern world, it is imperative to take time out for ritual.

As young children, the milestones we celebrated were steps to independence. The rituals reflected this, with the focus on just the child. As our perspective shifts we find that many rituals are connected to, or shared with, other people. This is in part because the adult world is more inter-dependent. Children are protected by the family from the outside world. The adult world is the outside world. So it is natural for these rites to reflect more of a world view. Bringing into them a new awareness of this great web of life, the adult Rites of Passage involve a different texture and depth. Here is a map for a way of life. There is no real sense of chronology from this point, except for the magick of turning twenty-one. This gives us the title of "adult" in society's eyes.

There is another magick of the adult world. Many rites will be repeated for some of us. Each time we move into a new home, each new relationship, each career choice, each new child, reflects another step in our growth. These experiences are what adulthood is all about. Choosing to celebrate them or not will shape our way of living. When we make the choice to celebrate, we underscore the growth and share the wonder with those around us. When we ignore those experiences and let them go by unnoticed, we rob ourselves of a chance to feel the magick in each part of life itself.

FIRST UNION

Under a full Moon in May, a young couple go off to the woods to share their first lovemaking together. The village shaman initiates the woman-child into full womanhood. Beneath the statue of the Goddess, a temple priestess shows a young man the arts of lovemaking. All are romantic notions based, in part, on history.

Two teenagers, very much in love, decide to "go all the way" while their parents are away for the weekend. They exchange rings in token of their relationship. Peers in school tease them, more out of envy than morality.

Two girls in school smile at each other. They begin to see each other after school and on weekends. There is a bond between them and they recognize the love in each others' eyes. Proudly they become lovers, finding warmth and strength in their choice.

Young men walk arm in arm down the street. They glow with the signs of new love. Their laughter lightens the Air around them, and some rejoice with them for this wonderful gift of fulfillment.

A young boy hardly speaks to anyone at home or in school. He is withdrawn and always looks sad. He fears the night, because that is when one of his family robbed him of all choice and control of his body.

A fifteen-year-old girl leaves school to have an unwanted baby. Two years later, she is working the streets of a major city. Her child will bear the scars of her unwilling initiation into sex.

There are many Rites of Passage. Not every Rite is warm and friendly.

In a society where sex is often referred to as lovemaking, it seems ironic and unfair that so many are introduced to sex against their will, or under a veil of guilt. Perhaps even more cruel are the lies that so often surround these beginnings. The first taste of sexuality should be fun and joyous, not fraught with threats. Lovemaking should be just that, an act of love, not of violence. Yet these are the realities of our world. We must find a way to celebrate a first union, and a way to heal those that have been robbed of dignity and choice.

There are, unfortunately, no spells to change what has been done. When a child or adult has been violated sexually, we must offer healing and unconditional love. For those who have been hurt, it would be better to first do a short ritual to allow the anger and tears to flow. Perhaps a Circle of those people closest could then provide a safe place in which the emotions that have been locked up inside could be released. The anger could be expressed, and the sense of guilt felt by the child/adult who was not responsible could be relieved. Too many who have been victimized in these horrible ways never forgive themselves for an act for which they are not responsible. Ritual is a good place to allow that shift in perspective to occur. When the tears have stopped, there should be food and drink to share. Everyone present should reaffirm the strength and beauty of the person who has found new inner strength. Sharing this way cannot undo the past, but it may allow the past to remain in the past, and pave the way for a stronger, more unified future.

Many adults may have two or more first unions that can be celebrated. There are so many of us who believe that we are identified sexually one way or another not out of choice, but out of a serious lack of choice. When we are finally able to express our true sexual preferences, that must be celebrated.

What of this new generation, these youths that have been raised in a more magickally enriched world? How do we avoid transferring our mixed feelings to them and retain their rights to privacy? We are a very long way from having a hillside set apart at our gatherings to let them re-enact the old Maypole rites. How do we help them celebrate this new experience? One possible solution comes from open communication. Long before the puberty rites, our children have been taught about safe sex, and freedom of choice. They are well informed and as prepared as we can help them become. After the puberty rites a parent or close adult friend might give them a sealed envelope. Inside there is a letter. When they are ready to have sex, or just after their first time the letter should be opened. In the letter thoughts about the adults own first experience, their own feelings of these new emotions and sensations are discussed. There is also a short meditation for them to consider.

> The Goddess and God have given us many blessings in this world. We are Their children. When two people are joined in an act of love, the magick of the stars is theirs to feel, and the beauty of the Earth is theirs to know. Remember these, and each act of love will grow upon the last, and you will be all the richer. Blessed be.

Once the envelope is given to the youth, we are done. It is not our place to ask if it has been read or opened. My experience has shown that when this kind of trust is demonstrated, the respect and trust are returned in the form of healthy, loving young adults.

JOBS AND FINANCIAL RESPONSIBILITY

Our ancestors were not as confused about adulthood as we are today. In their time, the passage of puberty and first sexual union meant one was considered a full adult in the community. Looking for a job, moving out of their parents' home, acquisition of material goods, these were all integrated into everyday life. As a child they learned a skill and as an adult they began to apply that early knowledge and skill in a tangible way. Their home was often built by other members of the village, and they were gifted with most of the things that they needed to begin life on their own. We need to evaluate this in light of our modern world.

Today we have Rites of Passage that our ancestors would never have needed because we are expected to assume *individual* responsibility in ways unknown to our ancestors. There is a point at which the paper route of childhood gives way to working in a convenience store. Babysitting is left in favor of office work or homemaking. Your neighbors' lawn is mowed by a younger kid down the street, and you try your hand at sales. Each time we begin a new job, regardless of what it is, we add new skills to our resume. No lessons are learned without some sort of future application. Our ancestors did not have these experiences. We live in a complex world that frowns on following in the footsteps of our families. It is a rare child who goes into the family business. Faced with so many options, we feel an obligation to try each option that presents itself.

Even the very act of seeking employment is more complex than it has ever been. We enact the ritual of reading the classified pages, and making the follow-up phone calls. We don our ritual clothing, of suits and dress shoes, our costumes fitting the image we wish to present. Forms are filled in with all the precision of ancient rites, and even the "interview" has the feel of a sacred mystery play re-enacted. Not all rituals must be held within a Circle.

By looking at the entire process this way we can begin to superimpose our own rituals on our daily lives and find a way to live in both worlds. When we are successful with that shifting of reality, then we truly perform magick.

With that thought in mind, as we prepare for the interview, we view ourselves in the job that we are seeking. In the past, talismans might have been used for safe travel or to ease a situation. We can do the same today. Cinquefoil, or five finger grass in our right shoe replaces older, more complicated rites. We "put our best foot forward" by entering the building with our right foot first. Our language reflects a tone that says that we already have the job, and we ask questions about how to proceed. Once we have the job itself, the cinquefoil goes into a small bag along with other herbs such as lavender (for attraction of positive attitudes) and dill weed (for tranquility) and sits in our desk.

Having viewed this modern "hunting rite" this way we understand why it is an important Rite of Passage. The first paycheck that is ours to spend as we choose becomes the final step and the reward for all of the work that has gone before.

INDIVIDUAL RESPONSIBILITY

Telephones are a modern convenience. In other times there were couriers, or those who knew the mystery of feathers, leaves and rocks and could send them to relay a message. Bards carried sacred songs, and troubadours the news, from town to town. Now, Ma Bell (a new Goddess in technological disguise?) makes it possible to do all this from our homes, offices and street corners. Unlike the Bardic College where the training was for transmitting sacred information, or the troubadours who learned to place news into song, the telephone has no way to screen or to qualify the messages carried through its electrical and laser nerve system. It becomes a matter of personal responsibility to open our awareness and to see a telephone as a sacred tool. If we take just a moment the first time we have one installed and ask for the blessings of Hermes, for example, to help to remind us of these attitudes, perhaps we would use our communicative skills with more compassion and honesty. Each time our phone rings, we are again reminded that magick takes place in more ways than we often think about. Having a small shrine near the phone will further enhance these thoughts each time we use the tool given to us by modern technology. To us this is just as important a tool as the plow was in its own time. In the future, our great-grandchildren may come to think of our tools as quaint and romantic. Magick itself is not restricted by our time.

Once it took days or weeks to move between two places.

Now we can do this in only a few hours. Cars have helped to shrink our immediate worlds. When we are given license to drive (and very often our first car), we are also given permission to no longer be bound to only one location. This freedom carries with it a new accountability to those around us. The very act of driving requires that we abide by a new set of rules. The card in our wallet confers upon us the title of adult. It will be used not only to allow us to drive, but will also serve as a form of identification. It is legal, it is real. By holding that card, we are validated in the eyes of society around us. This is the first time in our society that we actually are given tangible evidence of our new status in the world. Yet even with this, we are still not really a full adult (unless we have waited beyond our twenty-first birthday, at the least).

Now we ask if this is much different than giving a youth in another time her/his first horse. The answer must be "no." The effect is the same, only the technology has changed. We are saying to this generation, "you are free to move about, and are responsible to follow new rules." In today's world, then, we need to view this as a ritual of growing. It is time for a celebration. You might wish to follow some folk traditions of placing a red ribbon inside the car to protect the car from negative influences (e.g., mechanical failure), or you might put a small image on the dashboard and ask for the blessings of a particular deity or spirit. Cars can be a very personal thing. Shifting perspective and seeing this as a living Rite of Passage returns us to a feeling of real growth and helps the new driver to assume responsibility more easily, and with a deeper meaning.

A voice of majority is another major Rite of Passage in today's world. When I was younger I marched and petitioned for the 18- year-old vote. Today it is a reality, but one that often is taken for granted. Voting is not an isolated act that is performed only once annually. The right to vote carries with it a responsibility to be aware of options, possible changes, and pending decisions in our world. Pulling that lever today is one remaining link to the village meetings of cultures that have all but disappeared. When we take an active role in decisions, when we accept our responsibility to act upon our ethics, we re-connect with our grandparents and follow their example. The voter registration card is not only identification and proof of age, it is a symbol of our own concerns for the world around us and a token of our adulthood.

NEW HOUSE/FIRST HOUSE

It is no accident that the acquisition of a car is often the precursor to leaving ones' home. Today's society is mobile. It is the norm rather than the exception for young adults to leave the area in which they spent their childhood. Many young adults will test this freedom by going to colleges far away. They will practice independent living for the next four years. Most families move several times while they endeavor to make a better life for themselves. Corporations often pay to "relocate" employees, rather than to train new people from a local area. There is almost a militant attitude about *not* living where you were born.

How then do we rationalize this within the context of a spiritual path that places so much emphasis on home and hearth? How far can memory be stretched back to encompass a nomadic existence?

We all share a need to make *any* dwelling feel like it is more than just four blank walls. We use our homes for more than mere physical shelter; many of us set aside a room as a temple, a place in which to connect with the Gods. Many of us recognize the magick done in the kitchen and at the hearth. There is no place in the space in which one lives that is not sacred, that is not a place in which one can spend precious moments. The following ritual is a blessing that will create a bond of warmth between the new house and those about to live a good deal of their lives therein. It can easily be adapted for a single room in a roommate situation, or for a dorm room. It is written to be performed by a family, by room-mates, or by a single occupant and her/his friend(s). You will need:

A loaf of good bread—to keep your home from hunger.

Salt—a traditional symbol of law, here used to bring harmony and balance.

Wine/Juice—to represent bounty, love, and nurturing.

Candles—one for each room. Either use all white, or colors that express each room's use (see color chart in Appendix III).

New broom—to keep your new home free from past upsets.

An iron key that does *not* fit anything you own—iron for protection, a key that fits no keyhole to confuse those who would enter uninvited.

One yard of red ribbon—traditionally, the color red wards off evil.

Sachet bags—one for each window (each bag should contain dill seed, lavender and lotus root).

A Brigit's Cross—a traditional Irish symbol of the Goddess Brigit, made of reed or rushes. Many Irish or Celtic specialty shops sell them, and they are easy to make if you live in an area where reeds grow.

Sweep the house thoroughly using an old broom before beginning the ritual. While sweeping, visualize all residual energies of the previous occupants being gently pushed out. Imagine a sense of freshness, an emptiness like a quiet audience waiting for the musicians to begin.

In addition to sweeping for psychic cleansing, the house should be cleansed of any dirt or unwanted items (such as the ugly torn green and pink sofa left by the previous tenants). The ritual supplies should be placed in a basket outside near the door, and will be carried into the house before furniture or any other items are brought in. The new occupant begins the ritual in the kitchen with guest or co-habitants joining in.

New Occupant: I place this Brigit's Cross in my kitchen to bring warmth and solace, good company and lasting friendships. *(The cross is placed on the kitchen wall.)*

Occupant/Guest: Bread is the gift of the harvest. Good bread, like a good harvest, assures that you are never hungry or without blessings.

Occupant/Guest: This salt is here to remind you always of Nature's Law, for Nature is the provider of all things rich and good. May your home always be filled with riches.

Occupant/Guest: Wine is a symbol of life's perpetual cycles. Let us leave this wine here unopened, as a reminder of the wheel of the year. Like the fruits housed in this bottle, may your life here know bounty through change.

Occupant/Guest: These candles transform the darkness and light our way. May this home be a place of enlightenment and love. May passion dwell here.

Occupant/Guest: A new home is filled with new potential. Happy memories are welcomed here, unhappy memories cast aside. As you sweep this home clean, clear away unwanted memories, and always make room for bright beginnings. *(Presents broom.)*

Occupant/Guest: *(Tying the red ribbon to the top of the key.)* This key is placed on the front door to ward off any who would do harm here. May this home be a place of protection and safety.

The guests or children now place the sachets in all of the windows. They hang there to protect the home from sorrow, and encourage a harmonious psychic atmosphere. You might color coordinate them with each room.

After the sachets are hung, the participants share the bread and salt, and then a meal. This custom comes from the Celts, who believe that those who share bread and salt will never do harm to one another. The remaining salt, wine and candles should be put someplace safe and left there to ensure their continued blessing. It is a good idea to change the sachets once a year, as well as to "re-bless" the home. I like to do this around Candlemas (February 2) as a way to prepare for spring.

The Brigit's cross on the hearth wall, the key on a red ribbon hung on the door, and the sachets on the window sills all serve as a visual reminder, from day to day, of this blessing. Each time you see the first gifts brought into this house, they will strengthen the boundaries and psychic bonds you made through this ritual. The magick of everyday takes form here, as the wine reminds you of the wheel of which we are all part.

SELF-DEDICATION

Living on our own, we make decisions about our own spirituality. Our children draw their own conclusions about deity as well. Perhaps you have come to understand yourself better by incorporating the Goddess and God into everyday life, or your children, having been raised in this way, wish to make a more formal commitment to follow this path. It is time to consider a self-dedication.

The name can be misleading. Self-dedication simply means that you are dedicating yourself to a lifestyle of personal attunement with the Gods and Goddesses, nothing more. Although this is a self-dedication ritual, it does not mean that you must or should perform it alone. This ritual celebrates the affirmation of a life-path, and is given more depth when shared with those who are part of our Circle family. Affirmation and commitment are serious and binding, but this is not an initiation. To be initiated implies a mentor relationship with someone who already has had these experiences and has agreed to guide you in your own growth. Self-dedication is an important step, something to be regarded with respect. It is not a less significant ritual than others, nor is it lower on some vague ladder of spiritual growth. It also does not mean that you cannot move on if at some point initiation becomes an option for you, or that a self-dedication ritual would be inappropriate if you have been initiated. This ritual is something between you and the Gods and your invited guests.

The Ritual

If this ritual is being performed by a teen raised in the kind of spiritual home described throughout this book, then the details might be somewhat different than if this is to be done by an adult who has chosen this path after living on one or several other paths first. Once again, what is presented is only an outline of possibilities and the exact wording, staging and parts will need to be altered as necessary.

Friends and loved ones gather at the ritual site. There should be decorations to fit the season and the personality of the dedicant. The altar is set with candles for the Goddess and God, and symbols of the four directions. There is also food and drink to share.

Sweeping and Blessing the Circle

Maiden: *(Sweeping.)* This Circle is a place of love and commitment. We sweep away all feelings of doubt and anxiety. Let this space be filled with happiness and sharing, as we all join hands. Blessed be.

These parts may be performed by the dedicant or shared with those in attendance. It works either way, but the feeling is very different.

Dedicant: Creatures of Water, Children of the West, remove all feelings of what would cloud our thoughts. Replace them with confidence and clarity of purpose. Blessed be.

    Creatures of Salt, Children of the North, we ask that your blessings of integrity and inner strength be our blessings here today. Blessed be. *(Mixing the salt in the Water.)* As we blend these two elements, we ask that all here find inner balance within themselves. So mote it be.

Elemental Blessings

Each of the four elements (Air, Fire, Water, Earth) are to be passed around the Circle by all those in attendance. The dedicant should begin by first stating what it is that he/she would ask from each of the elements. As the element is passed, the next person should repeat the request from the person preceding her/him and add one of her/his own. This will continue around the Circle with all four elements, with each person (except the dedicant) stating two things. For example, if the dedicant begins in the East, Air, with "inspiration", the next person might say, "inspiration, renewed visions." The following person, "renewed visions, innocence", and so on around the Circle.

Calling the Quarters

Since we are here to celebrate a dedication to this spiritual path, the Quarters should be invited by the dedicant. These invitations should be stated as a request of a very honored guest to witness the oaths that will be made here in the Circle.

East: Spirits of Air, Brothers and Sisters of the East. I ask you to join in the Circle and share in my joy and new-found self. Bring with you the gift of the early morning song. Welcome.

South: Spirits of Fire, Brothers and Sisters of the South. I ask you to join in the Circle and share in my love of this world. Bring with you the gift of friendship's laughter. Welcome.

West: Spirits of Water, Sisters and Brothers of the West. I ask you to join in the Circle and share

in my dreams made manifest. Bring with you
the gift of our Mother's tears and the music of
a seashell. Welcome.

North: Spirits of Earth, Sisters and Brothers of the
North. I ask you to join in the Circle and
share in my inner strength. Bring with you
the gift of constancy and life ever renewing.
Welcome.

Calling the Goddess and God

Dedicant: Mother Earth, Heart Sister. You whose name
has been sung from the stars and whispered
on the winds. Join in this Circle and share my
heart's deepest joy. Welcome.

Father Sky, Dream Brother. You whose name
has been known in the oldest forests and
spoken from the highest rocks. Join in the
Circle and share my dedication. Welcome.

We have come together in this Circle to share
in my self-dedication to the God and Goddess. The presence of my family makes this
even more special to me. I thank you all for
being here to share and give honor to this
rite.

Offerings

Here a special family member or friend may walk with the
dedicant to each Quarter, or the dedicant may go to someone
in each Quarter who will read the meditation and present the
gifts. The gifts suggested may be altered to suit the specific
needs of the Dedicant and the Circle members.

East: Here is the East. The incense that you smell
reminds you of all the flowers of the fields,
where the songbirds have always sung the
sacred songs. Each breeze that you feel, each
word given life, has been drawn from here.
What promise would you make to the East?

Dedicant speaks her/his promise.

Accept this feather to remind you of what you
have promised here today. Blessed be.

South: Here is the South. The flame on this candle
reminds you that all life is nurtured by the
Sun and made manifest through the gifts of
love. Each time you are touched by warmth
or feel passion rise within you, know that here
is where they first began. What promise
would you make to the South?

Dedicant speaks his/her promise.

Accept this new candle to remind you of your
promise and your own potential. Blessed be.

West: Here is the West. The Water in this bowl
reminds us of our Mother's womb and the
unconditional love first offered us in this
world. Each time you feel the kiss of Water,
or your own heart fills with love or sorrow
and tears flow, you are a part of this beginning. What promise would you make to the
West?

Dedicant speaks her/his promise.

> Accept this seashell to remind you of all of
> life's beautiful beginnings. Always remember
> that you are a part of the cycle that never
> ends. Blessed be.

> North: Here is the North. The stone I hold
> reminds us of the strength and hidden wis-
> dom of the Earth itself, the soil of life's
> constant potential. When you walk upon our
> Mother, and see the grass and trees or taste
> the foods She has given to us, you are once
> again a part of the Earth. What promise
> would you make to the North?

Dedicant speaks his/her promise.

> Accept this stone as a symbol of your own
> new foundation. Blessed be.

Now the dedicant comes to the center and faces the Goddess
and God candles.

Circle member: These candles represent the God and
Goddess. Their love is like this flame.
Without the candle to sustain it, the flame
will die. Without your constant love and
seeking for the Gods' presence in your own
life, they will disappear from your world.
Look for Them in all things around you,
and remember to honor the Goddess and
God by living to your fullest potential.
What promise would you make to Them?

Dedicant speaks her/his promise.

> Accept these gifts. The bell is to remind
> you to remain clear in your own purpose,
> and the mirror is to allow you to always
> find your inner self. Blessed be.

Wine and Cakes

Food and drink should be shared at this time. The blessings should be made here by way of a toast to the new dedicant. Each guest should speak a few words and as the food is taken a libation should be made to honor the day. When all have had a chance to toast, stories, songs and gifts are shared.

Closing the Circle

You might choose to allow the candles to burn down or, if you extinguish them, they could be presented as a gift for the new dedicant's shrine.

Dedicant: Both Goddess and God have joined with us here to celebrate a new beginning. From Their never-ending dance I have found my own steps. As we end this Circle, and send Them home with a kiss, we ask that each of us find Their love in our lives. Blessed be.

East: Spirits of Air, Brothers and Sisters of the East. We thank you for being here with us and send you home with a kiss. Blessed be.

This is repeated for the other Quarters.

Dedicant: We all join hands once again before we leave here. Feel our unity and strength together. As we have come together as individuals sharing a common bond, we leave the Circle as individuals, yet always connected to each other. Blessed be.

The dedication opens many doors for growth and understanding. The ritual is not an isolated rite, to be performed and then forgotten. Having spoken these promises in the company of our Circle, a new layer of meaning, a deeper level of commitment has been added. In return, the Circle family now shares with the dedicant a responsibility to see that these promises are kept. By lending their energy at the beginning, they have also magickally stated their own willingness to help carry out the dedications. This ritual now makes it possible for the newly recognized responsibility to become fully accepted by the adult.

EMANCIPATION, OR TURNING TWENTY-ONE

The Rites of Passage that we have looked at so far all occur at random times. They await the readiness of the individual, and slowly help to transform the individual and lend a deeper meaning to his/her life. However, there is one rite that occurs whether or not a person is ready; it occurs at the stroke of a clock and the changing of a calendar page. Turning twenty-one is a shining example in today's modern world that "magick happens."

Suddenly, one who was a child in the eyes of the law, a mere minor with virtually no power, now has the ability to come and go as he/she pleases with no restrictions, but with full accountability in society. All of the adult trappings given earlier—the right to vote, the right to live independently, and the right to drive—are now celebrated with the purchase of the first legal drink. We are fully emancipated.

Purchasing alcoholic beverages is one of the only remaining signs left of this transition. The other changes are more subtle. Many will graduate from college in the same year, entering the work force or; choosing to move on in the academic world, they will take more control of their course of study. Some will do both. We need to find a way to mark this particular birthday and recognize the inner significance.

The previous few years were in some ways, a dress rehearsal for this. I don't think the ritual here takes place inside "sacred space," rather it takes place in the world itself. I would much prefer to see the acknowledgement of emancipation come from the individual who turns twenty-one. An open letter to friends and family stating positive actions to be taken to demonstrate adulthood would hold more meaning than walking across some esoteric bridge. Cutting a cord between child and parent also seems harsh to me, though I have seen rituals of this nature performed. In lieu of cutting a cord to show full emancipation, why not a shake hands to demonstrate partnership? (See the discussion of Handfastings for a more detailed ritual of this nature.) I look forward to a time when my children have grown into interesting adults and we can share a different level of understanding. Twenty-one may in fact be the time to remind our children that although they have grown, they are still our children, and we can still be a mentor for them in many ways.

6

BETROTHALS AND HANDFASTINGS

If you tell me you have found beauty here, then I will tell you it is only your own reflection you have found. Your eyes shine back at me with a glow that touches my deepest places. I treasure you above all others, and most honored to call you "friend."

—from a handfasting vow

A couple meet and magickally fall in love. That is the only way to describe what happens. When they look in each others eyes they find a reflection of their own dreams. Though each has been, and continues to be, an individual, they are complimented by something in this partnership. As they become comfortable with being a couple, a new need arises. A need to publicly declare the feeling of love for one another and to share this acknowledgement of commitment with family, friends and the Goddesses and Gods.

How long-term the commitment, and to what extent it is binding for the couple will be determined by the ritual used. There are major differences in the four rituals that follow. The betrothal is to acknowledge the love that binds the couple and to explore this love for the cycle of one year. One handfasting ritual is for as long as the love binds them together. In another handfasting ritual the couple states that they are to be together for this lifetime. And the last handfasting ritual, the most serious of all, speaks of an eternal bond that will span all lifetimes.

With the national divorce rates soaring, and with so many adults deciding to "live outside" of society as much as they can, these become difficult rituals to discuss. Our society offers many more options than those offered to our grandparents. To the dismay of some, there are many who feel that if there are any rules at all they should be to celebrate diversity, and convention be damned. In keeping with the tone set at the beginning of the book, I will outline these rituals from a so-called "traditional/conventional" perspective and write them for a woman and a man. As with the conception ritual, it is the intent and not the mechanics with which we are concerned. These rituals are meant to be adapted to the specific needs of a couple or a family, not to dictate policy.

BETROTHALS

A betrothal is performed when two individuals have made the decision to be joined together. Betrothals are drawn from a time in history when it was necessary for a couple to have children to ensure the continuance of the village or tribe. This was a ritual that committed the couple to stay together until a baby was born (approximately one year). Today's Betrothal makes a promise to try a relationship in a new way. Here is an opportunity to live as a couple, to share each other's joys and anguish, and to learn if in fact this is the "right" relationship to be part of. You might look at this as a sort of dress rehearsal for a future marriage. The ritual is a promise made publicly asking for the support of all those in attendance, and the blessings of both God and Goddess, but it is not yet a magickal act in and of itself.

Drawing from the imagery of a new life as the goal of this first year together, we will plant a seed as part of the rite itself; in an older society, a child would be born. Rather than planting an herb or flower that will grow for one year and never again, it is suggested to find a perennial that will grow year after year. If this is not possible for a city-bound couple, then a plant that can be grown indoors should be substituted. Any other symbol may be chosen by the couple as long as they feel that it will be a suitable substitute for the living object. Whatever is chosen should be something that they can nurture together over the course of time.

The Ritual

All invited guests should assemble at the ritual site. There should be decorations of the season and many flowers and fruits. In addition to a Priestess and a Priest to perform the ceremony, there should also be a couple to stand as witnesses. This particular couple functions much like a best man and maid of honor. They will witness the ritual and promise to act as confidant and support for the newly betrothed couple. Their vows will be spoken to the couple and should reflect the special relationship between them.

Casting the Circle

The salt and Water are blessed by the Priestess. All doubts are removed from the Water and they are replaced by security. The salt is blessed with the honor of all oaths taken. The joining of the salt and Water reminds us that when two things are joined as one they both change, but their union is a vital part of them both.

As the Circle is swept we see all the interferences of the outside world leaving the couple and make way for the couple to fulfill their own potentials.

Each element is passed from guest to guest asking for the blessings of Air, Fire, Water and Earth. Only one thought is stated aloud for each element as it makes its way around the

Circle. For Air we might ask for new dreams, Fire to bestow passion, Water for time to reflect and Earth for stability. The voices of all the guests add to the strength of these blessings, and allow all present to be a living part of the ritual.

Calling the Quarters should be performed by the two witnesses. They have a chance to ask not only for the presence of the Quarters, but also to add a personal flavor to those requests. As the Quarters are called, the guests face the appropriate direction and are invited to call upon the Quarters in their minds. This adds to the feeling of a family preparing for the celebration.

The Priest and the Priestess ask for the God and Goddess to join the Circle, calling the names most appropriate to the occasion and for the couple as well.

The Vows

With the Circle now complete we focus all attention toward the couple to be betrothed. All elements of the casting have been based upon them as individuals. Now, in this space cut away from the world of everyday, they make way for the beginnings of their lives united.

Priestess: You have come here today to state your love for one another in the company of your family and Goddess and God. We welcome you both.

Priest: Your eyes reflect the stars above and your smiles today hold each other's hearts. We all ask that this always be the way for you as you learn to grow together.

Priestess: When you look out in the world around you,

there are always things to remind you that no living creature is ever truly alone. The Earth supports all life, the Sun and the Moon watch us and light our paths. The stars above twinkle and smile for all to share, and the seas ripple in the winds. Your love is only one part of all those dances.

Priest: Perhaps you came to one another in a great flurry of love and adventure. Or maybe it was a calm growing love, slow and steady like the grains. No matter how you touched each other, no matter how your paths have brought you here today, it is your love that sustains the moment for all gathered in this Circle.

Priestess: _____ and _____, you have come both freely and gladly. What has brought you?

Couple: Our love for each other.

Priest: Have you brought a symbol of this love?

Couple: We have brought these seeds to be planted today.

The couple plant the seeds in a pot of fresh soil for all to see. The witnesses Water the seeds as token of their promise to help nurture the couple. As they do this they should also speak their promises aloud for all to hear.

Priestess: You have planted a seed in the Earth and also in each other's hearts. As you tend seeds in each other's hearts. As you tend seeds these remember to tend your partner. There will be times when you are filled with anger or fear; never let those thoughts go to sleep with you. Always strive to see the beauty that first touched you and the desire that has sparked your love.

Priest: Begin each day with a kiss and promise to find new ways to love. Learn to listen to the unspoken words and hear each other's meaning. Never let anger cloud your eyes or minds and forbid any violence to enter into your home.

Share music and laughter in all that you do and always remember that you are never truly alone.

Priestess: The vows that you take are meant only to be an aid for this next year. At this time you are not bound beyond that point. If you choose, you may then be Handfasted, but for now your promises are only these. Repeat them together:

I will walk with you through the Dance of the Thirteen Moons and together we will light a candle to mark the passing of each one. For this time I will be your lover and your friend, your confidant and your comforter. What load you carry, that load also will I carry. What need is your shall be my need. For you, I will open my hidden places, that your Sun

may shine on them. I will bring out my
treasures for you to love. I will be your mate,
sharing bread and salt with you. And at the
closing of the day, your body will be my
sleeping place, your shoulder my pillow.

For I have seen you and I love you.
You are walking in my soul.

When the Moons have crossed the Heavens
and the seasons all have witnessed our love;
then may we go on and be Handfasted. But
here and now I promise you one turning of
the wheel.

If you will have me, I am truly blessed by the
Gods with the fulfillment of my desires.

I love you.

If the couple has rings or other tokens they are exchanged at
this point.

The blessing of the Wine and Cakes should be performed
by the couple. Afterwards, gifts may be given and stories
shared.

When the time feels right, the Goddess and God are
thanked for Their presence and the Quarters are also thanked
and sent home with a kiss. The Circle has ended, but the lives
and love celebrated are only beginning.

*(These vows were written by Tamarra James and used here
with her kind permission.)*

The betrothal year has ended. We might choose to see this in modern terms as the end of the engagement period, when real marriage takes place. The vows to be taken are binding for as long as love lasts. There is strong magick involved as well. At the betrothal, a seed representing the couple was planted to be nurtured for a year. Now we take a moment to look at what has happened this union on a more subtle level. The seed needs further care. After a full year, there is the question of whether or not this union should continue. Can this relationship function? Were the vows of a year before easily adapted to a lifestyle, or was there a feeling of constant strife? Did family and friends offer support because of the love that continued to grow, or did they tend to leave because they could not be a party to this union? There was a time, not really all that long ago, when the marriage would be called off if someone saw a problem. What do the outward signs of those in the Circle of family and friends seem to indicate?

If everyone has agreed that this relationship is a good one, then it is time for the Handfasting. Ideally this will be the first of three different rituals to be performed over the lifetime of the couple. For now, we will look at a magickal bond that is for as long as love lasts.

The Ritual

As with the betrothal, all invited guests gather together to witness and to celebrate. If a seed was planted the year before, the plant should be brought into the Circle or a sprig of it should be placed on the altar. There might be rings to be exchanged. If so, they should occupy opposite ends of a wand, to symbolize the magick in the union. There should be a cord that will bind the wrists of the couple during the rite. If they so choose, a drop of each person's blood should be placed on the cord beforehand. Later this cord will be kept somewhere secure, to be used in later rites. If the witnesses of the betrothal are still involved in the lives of the couple, they should take on the same roles as they did during the betrothal. New witnesses would not change the outcome of the ritual, but when we are gifted with close friends we should cherish them and honor them in ways such as this.

Casting the Circle

Once again the casting of the Circle is based upon the lives and uniqueness of the couple for whom the ritual is being performed. All parts should reflect on them, and the parts should be taken by those family and friends who would lend them the most energy. The outline for the handfasting is the same as for the betrothal.

The real differences between the two rituals begin after the space has been defined.

Priestess: Welcome to all gathered here today. This is a place of love and family.

Priest: Welcome to all gathered here today. This is a place of growth and caring.

Priestess: _____ and _____, one year ago you stood in a Circle like this one and proclaimed your love for one another. Is that love still alive?

Couple: Yes.

Priest: _____ and _____, you have lived and loved for this year as partners. What have you learned?

Couple: *(Responds as desired.)*

Priestess: Together you have watched the stars and the Moon in their dance. You have felt the change of the seasons and with it you have felt each others love grow and transform. Knowing that with each passing of the cycle all things must change. Do you wish to remain together?

Couple: Yes.

Priest: Through this last year you have learned many things. Together you have begun a partnership of caring and nurturing. If you continue, will you also allow yourselves to grow in these ways?

Couple: Yes.

Priestess: When you were betrothed you did so for one full year. Now at the time of your Handfasting, will you promise to stay together for as long as your love lasts?

Couple: *(Responds as desire.)*

Priest: This Handfasting carries with it a magickal binding. Here in the presence of both God and Goddess, friends and family, you are weaving your two lives into one. Do you still wish to continue?

Couple: *(Responds as desired.)*

Priestess: Then place your right hands together. *(She ties the hands with the cord.)* Look into each other's eyes and find the reflection of your dreams made real.

Priest: *(Taking the incense.)* May all your days be blessed with the freshness of your love. As this incense is the breath of both God and Goddess, may the words that you speak always resolve in Their wisdom.

Witness: *(Taking the candle.)* May your lives be filled with great passions. This flame is not just the intense passion of a new love, it is the drive and desire that endures through time. Never lose your passion or lack for inspiration from one another.

Priestess: *(Taking the Water.)* May each day renew and refresh your love. Look upon this Water and remember that the tears of love may also burn your cheeks. Knowing this, when you have great sadness we ask that your love will ease the pains, and when you have great joy that your love will help it to soar.

Witness: *(Taking the salt.)* This salt is a promise to you both. Today you will speak vows to seal your love and your lives. As you grow stronger together and your vows take on newer and deeper meaning, this salt will be there to ensure that the gifts of the Earth are yours for all time. The richness it promises comes not in the form of money, but in the form of knowledge and compassion.

Priestess: Now we ask the Goddess and God to guide each of you, and that every day you find Their love for you in each other.

Priest: Now it is time for you to speak your vows aloud.

The couple exchanges vows that they have written for each other.

Witnesses: As you have both promised these things to each other, we make you these promises *(Speak promises to the couple as desired.)*

At this time other guests are invited to share any special blessings they that might have for the couple.

Priest: *(Holding the wand with the rings, or other token for the exchange.)* Your vows have now been heard by all. These rings, like your vows, are without beginning or ending. When you place them on your lover's hand, you have set a seal of your love and respect there.

Priestess: Wear these rings with great pride and always remember the love that brought you to-gether. *(She gives the rings to the witnesses, who help the couple place them each other's hands.)*

Priestess: *(Removing the binding cord and giving it to the couple.)* Your words have been said, your love has been proclaimed loudly. Now we share food and drink to celebrate the bounty of the Earth and the ever-present nurturing of all love.

The couple should bless the Wine and Cakes in their own words, since this is in effect their first meal as a handfasted couple.

During the blessing of Wine and Cakes, a broom is placed behind the couple. As soon as they have finished sharing the food, everyone shouts for them to jump the broom. This is to ask for fertility (creativity) in their lives. When they have jumped, they are chased out of the Circle, to be alone for a short time. While they are gone, the Circle is ended by the Priestess and the Priest in a manner suitable for the situation. This should be done quietly as the other guests set out a feast for all to share.

HANDFASTING: TILL DEATH DO US PART

Seven years have passed. The partnership of this marriage has found its own rhythm, defined its own patterns. The seeds of the Betrothal have grown. There are likely to be children present in the family. Careers are now a reality and there is a security that underscores each day. Even through times of stress and sorrow, this family has found a way to cope and to help each other through. When doubts about the marriage have set in, as they sometimes do, they have been met with dignity and caring, resolving in new ways to communicate. In our terms, this is a healthy marriage.

Our culture does not really allow for any celebrations to mark the kind of love that comes after time. This is more than just an anniversary on the calendar. The first years of family life are a short time, but long enough for a couple to truly know each other, for a new love to be born. Faults are accepted and understood, even if not always tolerated as well as we'd like them to be. At the seven year mark it is no longer the love of a couple, it is the love that has grown between family members. Now the celebration is for them, and not for the outside world.

The second handfasting is a statement of commitment to a family unit. The ritual is not held in a public place, it is held inside the home. There is no reason to cast an elaborate Circle here because the Gods and Goddesses need no formal invitation. Promises made during this ritual are for the sharing of this family only. The second handfasting is drawn from a time when the family was considered to be a happy productive unit, and when spiritual life was interwoven into everyday affairs. We take time to renew the vows made during the first handfasting, and add to them a vow that we will stay together for this lifetime.

Why here at seven years? Is it to ward off the seven year itch? I doubt that the original reasons for choosing this time are really known. Seven is the Chariot in the Tarot, the first Initiation, a card that relates to speech and the sanctity of the spoken word. Many words will have been spoken at this point in a marriage, and the taking of new vows will have far deeper meaning in light of these thoughts. Maybe it stems from a time when children were more a part of a marriage. This ritual is a way of ensuring your children that you will stay together for this lifetime. It is another way of saying that you intend to be together to raise them. However our ancestors decided on the timing, it is a wonderful celebration for the family.

What of those of us who have chosen not to have children? Is this ritual still important? The validation that we give to our partners and to our relationship in this ritual is vital. Though based on the idea of raising a family, this in no way excludes those whose lives are as full and rich without children. The purpose here is to acknowledge that after time has passed, we are able to make a better decision about remaining in this relationship for this lifetime. Now the promises made are for the two lovers and all that their marriage has come to mean to them. Now they must celebrate the fruits of the seeds planted for themselves so long before. This is a time of empowering one another and of remembering the love that first brought them together.

The Ritual

Both partners have thought about the new vows that they would like to take. Sitting with the family in a special place in the house reminds all involved that this is for them. Flowers should decorate the room or table and candles should be lit to help separate this from other family gatherings. The cord used at the handfasting also should be present.

I like to use a small fire, which can easily be managed indoors by placing rubbing alcohol inside a pyrex bowl and lighting it. Drambuie may be used for the Fire and the warm honey-flavored drink can be shared by everyone. Or you may simply use a candle. With the flames burning, the vows are spoken to each other. The partners place a knot in the handfasting cord, and add one for each child. Then, holding the cord over the flame (but careful not to burn the cord!) words to this effect should be spoken:

> Together seven times we have watched the
> changing of the seasons. There have been
> tears of joy and sorrow between us. The
> dreams that were once mere reflections in
> your eyes have grown and become manifest.

> Love and respect have become a way of life
> for us. When I look upon you I see my lover,
> my partner and my friend. Calmness has
> come with the passage of time, and I am
> ready to ask you to be with me for this
> lifetime. I love you.

A special meal should be shared by the family. If it seems right, you may invite several close friends to come and join you, but this ritual is traditionally done only by the couple and children because the magick is for them.

HANDFASTING: "TO LIVE AND KNOW, AND LOVE AGAIN"

Twenty-one years have passed. The seeds planted so long ago have grown and matured. The roots have reached deep touching things that could have only been guessed at in the beginning. The branches have expanded far beyond horizons that once were only dreams. The cycles of harvest and loss are no strangers here. Nor have the blessings of new growth been without number. What was begun in love has now blossomed and matured.

Some say that after so long a time a couple has reached their twilight years and that their marriage has grown predictable. If that were true, why then do so many look to the Sunset, eagerly anticipating inspiration each day? With the blessings of maturity partners can look at one another and understand who they are. This is a point of reflection. Granted, every relationship will have a fair share of lost dreams and missed opportunities, but there are far more things to be counted as gifts and blessings. After twenty-one years, the richness that can be found deserves to be celebrated and enjoyed.

We live in a youth-oriented society, where the thought of

growing older is devalued and dreaded. We are told that "nothing lasts forever" in tones that would have us believe that there is no hope, no deep purpose to anything. This simply is not the case. Love can be and often is, forever. With the understanding that comes from a lifetime shared, the family may feel that this is only a continuation of times that have come before. Through the eyes of experience and love, a larger picture may become clear. The third handfasting is a way to mark this point in time.

Our children have grown by this time. We look upon these young adults and cannot help but see them as our babies. Yet another glance reminds us that they are no longer small children. The promises made during the second handfasting have been kept, and we are preparing for our children to leave home. Of course we are glad of their independence, but we must also adjust to once again living as a couple alone. This is also well marked in the third handfasting.

Unlike the other rituals, this is a statement of faith beyond what we can see or even catch a glimpse of in this lifetime. This is a ritual where we ask to be bound to the one we have shared this life with for all lives. There are no promises made as to how that sharing will be determined in the future (or the past, if you don't express time as linear). The dynamics we understand in this marriage may or may not repeat themselves in another life. Love itself is not bound to rules of "acceptable" relationships as defined in this culture. So, here is the ultimate ritual of love and faith. In further demonstration of this, the ritual is officiated by our children. Here we see a living reminder of the ever continuing cycles of life and love. These children, borne out of the love of the union, now tie the final knot in a ritual gesture that says that love will always continue once it has been allowed to begin.

The ritual itself can be the same as the very first handfasting. There are only a few words that need to be changed to reflect the passage of time. (If the couple has no children, then it would be the honor of their oldest and dearest friends to perform this ritual.) The original binding cord should be used and then knotted to form a circle. Later the couple should choose to plant it in their garden or make it part of an offering to the Earth, another demonstration that all things change and are still connected to each other.

Having our children marry us allows us to see them as adults and helps to bind the family in ways that can only be described as magickal. They are now the active ones in the Circle and we, having done our job well, are rewarded by being allowed to participate and teach, sharing the wisdom of our life's experience. With this also comes the freedom to return to a relationship as lovers on a deeper and more subtle level. The third handfasting is not to be performed lightly. It should be performed with great joy and honor.

7

WISDOM ATTAINED

The paths you have walked have presented you with many
options. Your life has been rich with experience, and filled
with both sorrow and joy. Your teachers have gone on, and
now you must assume their role. There are many who look
to you now, eyes filled with wonder, hearts open, ready to
learn. Now you must decide whether or not to honor your
own teachers by following their steps. You possess more than
just the answers. You have learned the questions.

—from a traditional elder ritual

Graying hair. Wrinkled faces. Eyes that have seen the passing
of many seasons. Signs of wisdom, or signs of a life now spent?
Revered teachers, or dispensable population? Our responses
reveal much about our values as individuals, and as a society.

I often hear people lamenting the loss of our grandmothers
and grandfathers. "Where are our great teachers?" they say.
"Gone." Yet I see, senior citizens walking about on the streets
of every city and town, seemingly lost. Aren't these our
grandparents? Must a person's ancestry seem exotic to us in
order for there to be value inherent in a lifetime of experience?
Logic tells us "no," but this is not always the case. Our culture
tends to ignore this segment of our population, and our own
fears of growing older help to reinforce these ideas on a
subconscious level. The time has come for us to reclaim our
elders as revered teachers and respected members of society.

The point at which a person is considered wise is not to be

found on a calendar, nor is it found when certain physical changes become obvious. How and when we choose to acknowledge the wisdom we have gained in our lifetime is a personal decision. Cultures that have relied on menopause as the point of delineation for women or the graying of hair for men, seem to suggest a form of reverse puberty ritual. Although it could be argued that these physical changes are a very important part of growing older, neither in and of itself is truly an indication of insight or wisdom.

There are ways to honor wisdom without necessarily relying on purely physical manifestations. Here we must be ready to notice a subtle shift in ourselves (or our elders) and mark this passage. Some may choose to call this a "Croning" for women and an "Eldering" for men. In the tradition with which I am familiar it was simply an acknowledgement of wisdom attained. There was no great amount of fanfare, just a quiet recognition of the work of a lifetime. A shift in roles occurs from open-ended teaching to a mentor relationship. This was a time for taking on apprentices, for focusing attention on those in the family Circle who were most interested or best suited to a specific skill that one possessed. There were in fact no written ritual celebrations. These events were marked in a natural flow of events for the family. The fact that an apprentice had been taken under wing would be announced at a family dinner or other gathering. Artificial tokens were not given in the form of gold watches, but respect was clearly evident and the good name that goes with that is far more valuable.

The traditions to which I refer were part of a continuum of ritual that spanned a lifetime. Many who have found that rituals make a dramatic difference in their lives may not have been as fortunate to have celebrated various milestones. For those who have joined us here, at a quieter time in life, it is fitting that we have a way to offer a place for reflection and consideration. Our modern rituals are based in the wealth of tradition left to us, and reflect a lifestyle that is vastly different from that of our grandparents. What makes celebrating Rites of Passage so wonderful, and comprises the single most important factor of ritual, is the constant growth that is found throughout them all. We use a symbolic language that may differ from others, yet the underlying reasons are the same now as they have always been, to re-link ourselves with our past, and thereby to make a commitment to our future.

CRONING

When a woman has passed her childbearing years and has found her own inner self, it is time to consider doing a Croning ritual. Many will choose to perform this ritual to coincide with menopause. Others will see this as a way to mark the transition to grandmotherhood, even for women who have not borne children. This would follow the traditions of Native Peoples, who view all elder members of the tribe as grandparents.

An important fact to be remembered is that no matter what means have been employed to determine the timing, the ritual will more than simply growing older. There is much emphasis on the passage of time within one's life as well as on the place of an individual life within the greater cycle of all life. This is a time for women to gather and celebrate together. After the ritual is over, it is good to invite men into the group and to share in the stories and feasting. The Circle roles are:

The Crone: This is the woman for whom this ritual is being held. She is the guest of honor and revered celebrant.

Maid: This is a young girl, perhaps a granddaughter or a niece, who represents the potential with which life begins.

Mother: The nurturer in all women is found within the Mother. She is the symbol of life's many forms of bounty. This may even be the daughter of The Crone.

Grandmother: This is one who has already been recognized by the family as an honored teacher. She reminds us that with age comes many gifts, but that age still presents new paths for us to walk.

Casting the Circle

The Maid sweeps the Circle with a broom. This broom should be fashioned out of various twigs and grains that are meaningful to The Crone, and possibly tied with pieces of willow.

Maid: This Circle is a time for celebration. We sweep to make room for all new beginnings and to honor our pasts. Let all gathered here always remember the bonds that have brought us together. Blessed be.

Everyone standing in the Circle now join hands. They move about clockwise slowly chanting:

The Circle of life moves on. We are all part of that Circle. The dance of life goes round.

They stop after they have gone around the Circle three times.

Blessing with the Elements

Incense is taken from the altar and passed from one person to the next. A red candle follows for Fire, then a cup of Water and a dish of salt. As each element is passed, the participants are invited to name something about the element, to invite its blessings. For Air you might invite freedom, for Fire creativity, for Water reflection and for Earth wisdom.

Calling the Quarters

East: Spirits of Air come to us. We all greet you with open hearts and minds. Be welcomed here and share with our joy. Blessed be.

South: Spirits of Fire come to us. We all greet you with the warmth of our love. Be welcomed here and share in our celebration. Blessed be.

West: Spirits of Water come to us. We all greet you with the reflections of our collective dreams. Be welcomed here and share our visions. Blessed be.

North: Spirits of Earth come to us. We all greet you with the strength of our family bonds. Be welcomed here and share our community. Blessed be.

Inviting the Goddess and God

The Crone may choose to call upon the name(s) of the Goddess(es) and God(s) to whom she is most drawn. Since this is her ritual, and these are her honored guests, it is only fitting that this honor should be hers.

The Ritual

Grandmother: Sisters, we have gathered here today to share a moment, a moment frozen in time, to mark the passage of one time of life to another. Many here are younger, and for them this time of life may seem very foreign. Some may still fear the Crone that is part of life's cycle. But as I stand here before all of our family, I am not a foreigner, nor am I frightening. This passage is not a sentence of foreboding. It is a time of great freedom and rejoicing. We are here to give honor and love to _____, and by so doing to honor all of our grandmothers since time's beginning.

The Crone is now led to a seat in the middle of the Circle.

Maid: I am the Maiden both young woman and little girl. My constant questions led you to look beyond yourself and to find your own place in the world. Though you have long since left parts of your childhood behind, my presence here is for all the questions that you have yet to ask.

I offer you this daisy, as a token of your own childhood and as a token of the freedom to ask more questions, which you will always possess.

The Crone accepts the flower and may wish to speak to the Maiden.

Mother: I am the Mother. I have borne children and
           nurtured countless more. When those around
           you were hungry, it was my recipe for stone
           soup that helped to fill both bellies and hearts.
           Now you have walked beyond my garden, but
           the seeds that you have planted will continue
           to grow. Those seeds will still look to you for
           tending and caring. The things that you have
           loved will return that love to you.

           I offer you this tiger lily. Once planted it will
           grow for many years and seed the Earth
           around itself, and so will grow beyond its own
           lifetime. As you have nurtured and loved
           others, you too have planted seeds that will
           inspire those whose lives you have touched to
           nurture and love again and again.

The Crone accepts the tiger lily and offers words to the
Mother.

Grandmother: I am the Grandmother. Long ago you
              thought of me as far beyond your own
              lifetime. Now you, too, are older and wiser.
              As a child you looked to me for knowledge
              and strength. Now you must return those
              things that you sought to those who will seek
              them in you. Your life has been filled with
              richness and wonder. Time has granted you
              with a precious gift, patience. You now know
              that the seasons will follow in their own order
              and that there is always time enough to look
              around to find beauty.

I offer you these laurels. These are to remind you of all the great accomplishments that you have had during your life, and that all accomplishments are great. They are given to you as a sign of respect and honor, because your place in our family is cherished.

The Crone accepts the laurels and may wish to state her own hopes for what she will accomplish during this part of her life.

All members of the Circle now come forward one at a time and give a flower to The Crone to mark a special part of her life. As the flower is presented, each family member and guest states aloud why that particular flower was chosen. Some examples might be: a red rose for the first taste of passion; a gladiolus to remember that every year has at least one event that stands out more than any other, the same way the gladiolus stands tallest in the garden; wheat shafts for the nurturer, and so on. The symbolism and meaning need only make sense to those in the family. In this way, we gift The Crone with a bouquet of her life to hold in her arms. If silk flowers are available, you might also have a duplicate bouquet to present later. Or, perhaps when the flowers dry, they might be collected and placed in a glass jar with oils as a potpourri.

When everyone has presented her flower, food and drink should be shared.

Wine and Cakes

A basket of fruit and fresh bread is brought forward. A chalice filled with a blend of juices is also brought forward. The woman who has the closest relationship with The Crone may be given the food for the blessing.

> This food and drink is like the harvest of our
> lives. It is rich in its diversity. We give thanks
> to both Goddess and God, the rain and the
> wind for Their blessings. The Sun, the Moon
> and the stars all sang Their songs for these to
> grow, and that music is carried in all of our
> souls. Blessed be.

After the food and drink have been shared, stories may be
told. When the time feels right, it is time to end the Circle.

The Crone should bid farewell to Goddess and God. The
Quarters should be thanked by those who called them.
Before leaving the Circle, all join hands and move counter-
clockwise and chant:

> The Circle of life moves on. We are all part of
> that Circle. The dance of life goes round.

ELDERING

A transition occurs somewhere between being a father and
being a grandfather. Full time parenting gives way to long
afternoon walks and visits with friends and family. The
urgency of making a way in the world dissolves into simply
being in the world. Proving "manhood" and self-worth no
longer matter as much as being content with oneself. We call
this becoming wise.

For men in our culture, older age often means having to
give up a job. Suddenly, after years of working outside the
home we require our men to become full-time homebodies.
Even in the years directly preceding retirement, there is a very
clear change in the way "senior" members of the work force
are treated. All too frequently, younger workers begin to vie

for a position that is far from vacant. All of these things conspire to make old age seem less than desirable.

What became of mentorship in the work place? What of teaching the young? These positive nurturing male roles have been all but wiped out in modern America. An Eldering ritual is one way of restoring these vital role models, not just for our valued teachers but for our own sakes as well. By taking time to acknowledge these roles, we ensure our place in the cycle later on and connect with our parents and grandparents and great-grandparents once again.

Determining the proper time for an Eldering ritual is more difficult than for a Croning. Women bleed and then stop, so that is one way to judge when to do a Croning. Gray hair is a possible sign, but it is hardly foolproof. I believe that it is time for an Eldering when the call to teach one-on-one begins, or when younger members of the family and Circle begin to seek wisdom from one special male. There is much to be said here for not taking on a title until it has been bestowed upon you from the outside. The Circle roles are:

The Elder: This is the man who is to be honored. He is the focus of the ritual and all is done to share the feelings of love and respect the family holds for him.

Youth: From each man's own childhood comes the beginnings of his path. The Youth is the point of origin for each of us. He represents the first questions, the first discoveries. From these are developed the primary drives to make them worthwhile.

Dreamer: Inside every old man lives a young boy, the stories say. The Dreamer is that boy, whose seeking and wide-eyed searching reaches far beyond the stars.

Father: The desire to nurture and to protect those around him is only on aspect of the Father. One of our primary teachers, he is there to offer guidance and leadership. Teaching us to look for our own signposts, he adds the dimension of humor to everything we do and learn. By his example we are introduced to unconditional love.

Grandfather: Through eyes that have watched the seasons change, and a heart that has grown by being touched by the lives around him, the Grandfather completes the Circle. Within him are the experiences of a lifetime, the stories and lessons to be learned. He is the patient listener and teacher.

Casting the Circle

All gather in the ritual area and hold hands. A dish holding seeds is passed around the Circle.

Youth: These are our still sleeping dreams. Our
                hopes and aspirations of a lifetime. With these
                seeds we cast our Circle.

Each person drops a few seeds on the Earth. (If this ritual is done indoors, then you should soak the seeds in Water. Sprinkle the Water around the Circle and later plant the seeds outdoors.) When all have done so, the last person says:

    Our Circle is cast.

Blessing with the Elements

A symbol of each element is passed by all members of the Circle, and a thought is shared with each one. For example, as the element representing the East is passed you might say,

"I remember the first spring breeze," and for Water you might say, "Let all emotions be clear and celebrated here." By doing this all the participants help to create the Circle and include a part of themselves within it.

Calling the Quarters

East: Spirits of Air and Wit. We call you to our Circle. Join with us as we celebrate together and give honor to _____. Blessed be.

South: Spirits of Fire and Passion. We call you to our Circle. Join with us as we share our love and give honor to _____. Blessed be.

West: Spirits of Water and Dreams. We call you to our Circle. Join us as we share our visions and give honor to _____. Blessed be.

North: Spirits of Earth and Wisdom. We call you to our Circle. Join us as we share our family bonds and give honor to _____. Blessed be.

Calling the Gods and Goddesses

It is a privilege to call upon the Gods in a ritual space. This ritual is more than just a Rite of Passage for the Elder, it is a ritual for the extended family. Having the Elder call the Gods and Goddesses to the space that he would honor, is another way of sharing his special moment.

The Ritual

The Elder is now brought to stand in the center of the Circle. As each person speaks, they may come forward and hold hands with, or in other ways touch the Elder.

Father: I look into your eyes and find a reflection of myself. You have taught and nurtured those around you and enriched their lives. These are the things that I wish to do in my life. Will you teach me and guide me as others have taught you?

The Elder responds as desired.

Youth: I am young. My whole life is before me. Yet when I look into your eyes I feel a kinship with you and all the men who have been guiding me. There are many questions that I would ask you, things that need to be explained. You possess skills even my own father does not possess. May I learn from you and preserve our past for my own future?

The Elder responds as desired.

Dreamer: I dream. Watching the stars above, I find a pattern in their dance. Celebrating the seasons I rejoice as each tree buds and blooms and changes to begin again after its wintry sleep. Some say that I need to dream less and to work more. Your twinkling eyes tell me that it need not be that way. What secrets do you know that you can share with me?

The Elder responds as desired.

Grandfather: I stand here as a mirror for your soul. We are one of a kind, connected through the ages by our longevity. Too much has been lost to the past, locked away by those who were afraid of its power. We must not allow that to fall to our own sons. Our lives have been rich, we have worked hard. The surest way to preserve knowledge is by teaching others. Time has been good to us and now we can use that gift. Will you remember the stories and tell them often? Will you look beyond the stars and continue the dream?

The Elder responds as desired.

Grandfather: This gift of knowledge is not without its own rewards. All who are gathered here also have gifts for you.

The family members now come forward and offer a gift or promise to the Elder as a thank-you. They may choose to thank him for specific things that he has taught them, or for that something he may inspired in their lives. When everyone is finished it is time for food and drink.

Blessing the Food

Home baked breads, and fruits and cheese should be brought forward. Drinks should also be available for all to share. If there is a son present he should do the blessing. If not, someone who is like a brother should be chosen. If the family is fortunate enough to have a living grandparent, then this should be their honor.

> This food and drink are a gift of our Mother
> Earth. Together we all share in Her bounty.
> The Sky Father watched over this food and
> when we eat together we promise to watch
> over each other. May we always feel as close
> as we do at this moment. Blessed be.

Stories may be shared as the food is eaten. When the time feels right, the Circle should be ended. The Elder should thank the Gods and Goddesses, and the same people who invited the Quarters should now thank them.

Before leaving the area, all join hands one last time.

Youth: We came together to honor _____, and
           each other. As the seeds were our beginning,
           their growth reminds us that Circles are never
           broken and cycles never lost. We leave here
           now as brothers and friends. Merry part.

THE EMPTY NEST

Raising a family involves more than simply having children. It is, ideally, an expression of faith that there is a future. When we make a conscious decision to share a spiritual belief with our children, and include them in our Rites of Passage, we give them a gift of ourselves that will stay with them for their whole lives. Our homes are the places in which they will rehearse over and over again for a time when they will be ready to go off on their own. Most of us want our children to find happiness in the world and to live their own lives. Yet, when that happens the shape of our immediate world changes and we find ourselves suddenly blessed with that extra room we've always wanted. All too often this comes with a price tag reading depression.

In extended families there are not "empty nests" in the usual way that we think of them. Elders are cherished and it is considered an honor to share living space with one. The change in domestic status might come more in the form of giving the larger portion of the home to the younger family, and moving a few rooms away. Although still close to the family, the change in status still might cause some depression. We will not offer a cure for this phenomenon here.

Even those who choose to not have children will experience something akin to the "empty nest." While there is not a significant change in the members of a household, sometime in the later forties or early fifties life views shift. A new need for a quieter homefront will cause a shift in social habits. Perhaps it is instigated in the workplace. Jobs or promotions are often given to younger employees, and when cutbacks occur the Elders are often the first to vanish. Or, if you have been fortunate enough to have taken on an apprentice, then this might be the time when they are ready to leave you and go off on their own. So once again the impact of this passage, though vastly different in many ways, takes its own toll.

How we react to this time of change will have a lasting effect on the rest of our lives. When we view this change as an opportunity for new growth, we open the way for new growth to become a part of each day. But, when this is viewed with fear and resentment toward those who are younger, we open the doors to embitterment and sorrow. There is a strong need for us to see the inherent success in having raised our family (or in having trained an apprentice) well enough for them to go out into the world and find their own place.

One form of celebration might occur during the wedding ceremony of the last child to leave the home. In Jewish tradition this is called the "mizinka," and the mother is presented with a garland of laurels to wear. While guests are gathered at the wedding reception both the mother and the father are seated in the center of a circle. All of the guests dance around them. Everyone joins together as a community to congratulate the parents on a job well done. The dance is an outward expression of the parents' lives own cycles; the laurels represent victory and honor.

In families where a third handfasting has been performed, the transition to the empty nest has already begun. Even if there is no desire to have a ritual that is as magickally bonding, it seems reasonable to renew marriage vows when all of the children have left. This is a way for couples to recapture the excitement of the beginning of their marriage. This is often the first time in many years they will be living all alone. An additional honeymoon is a wonderful way to ritualize this new beginning.

No matter what else may be done to mark this change, the dynamics of the household will change. Walking into a room that had been occupied by a child only weeks before can be eerie. Books, tapes, furniture, kitchen supplies may all be missing, as well. The house feels different. Remembering when the house was new, and looking at the blessing performed back then, we take a cue and repeat the basic ritual, with a few modifications.

A Ritual For House Blessing

When we find ourselves living alone in a house after having shared it with our children, there is an emptiness in some of the rooms. This ritual is a way to reclaim those rooms for our own use, and to re-establish the home as a place for the couple.

Since the entire focus is on the couple, they may wish to perform this ritual on their own. Or, if they choose to have invited guests, they should be peers, not their children.

We begin by sweeping the house of all unwanted influences. Beginning with the room farthest from the door, the woman sweeps toward the opening, concentrating on removing past conflicts. This is repeated in all of the rooms until everything is ritually swept away. At this point the couple stands outside the doorway.

In a basket they have gathered bread (the symbol of nurturing one another), wine or juice (for their love), candles (symbolizing both romance and the hearth), fresh fruit and flowers (the bounty of a lifetime and the beauty of its sharing). They walk into the house together. They kiss as they enter. They carry the basket into each room, where they share a memory or a thought. Then each states aloud how he/she sees this room changing and becoming a better place for the two of them. When they have finished, the couple goes into their favorite room and sets the basket down. (If guests have been invited they, too, are encouraged to share thoughts about the house and the lives of the couple.)

Next, the couple takes a bath together. This gives them time to focus love and attention on their partner, bringing back the images of a conception ritual or other times when they had reason to ritually bathe. When they have finished, they return to the room with the basket. After lighting the candles, they share the food and drink and enjoy the flowers. (Guests might have actually set the feast for them during their bath.)

When the ritual has been completed, it is fun to go out and purchase something new for the house, to symbolize this time of new beginnings. Friends and family should respect the change in the status of the household and should allow some time to pass before resuming normal visiting patterns. There will of course be those couples who view this as a time for increased visits because they are no longer bound by the schedules of other family members. Paying attention to the signals given, and being aware of shifts in moods, will be the best guidelines.

BECOMING GRANDPARENTS

If having children can be viewed as an expression of belief in the future, then becoming a grandparent can be seen as that belief becoming manifest. It is a shame that this event is too often shared via the telephone and photographs, instead of actually being a part of the life of these children. This should be a time of linking the family's history together, and of teaching about the cycles of the world through the extended family. Grandchildren who are given the opportunity to know their grandparents have the advantage of seeing the world through the eyes of experience. In my own lifetime, my great-aunts (my own grandparents had passed on before I was old enough to enjoy them) would tell me stories about Russia and Romania. The world of which they spoke was as rich to me as any fairy tale, maybe better because the stories were real. From those stories I was able to understand a part of history in a way that textbooks could never reveal. Hearing about the ways in which my own ancestors had lived helped me to understand the ways in which my own parents related to me. Wisdom that comes with age was taught to me, a child. It was a way of saying that even though the world would change as I grew, this wisdom would not be lost.

There is a modern myth in the Craft community. It says that the Craft must skip a generation. What this means is that the Craft is taught from grandparent to grandchild. Parents are involved with the everyday affairs of the world. Grandparents are blessed with the time to teach. There is no greater job, nothing more important, than helping to shape the next generation.

The legacy of grandparenthood has too long been ignored. There are no rituals to capture its deep significance. The reason for this is simple. No ritual can compare with the magick and power of holding a new grandchild. The love that is there cannot be mimicked in a setting beyond the natural setting of that very first moment. Being involved with the child, teaching and sharing are magick and ritual enough for anyone.

The wisdom of a lifetime's experience is a precious gift. There are not as many milestones to mark during this time of life. Yet, when we reflect on all the milestones that have come before, they were so much richer when we included our elders. This is a time of life for sharing. Perhaps the lesson here is to strive to keep all parts of our lives in balance and to never lose sight of the beauty of the continuing circle of life.

8

TEARS OF SORROW

Your sorrow is real, your loss is great. It does not matter, for
now, how others have felt before you. This is your time, your
space in which to express anger and hurt. No one will
reproach you for the words you speak, or for the way you feel.
Allow yourself to explore these depths so that in time you may
once again know the heights of joy.

—my teacher's words

Every day is a mixture of joy and sorrow, gains and losses.
Most of the time we take each day as it comes, living to the
fullest some days and barely getting through others. We take
little note of the pluses and minuses on a daily basis. Then,
suddenly, something happens to change that balance. We
suffer a major loss, something so big that it cannot be ignored.
We grieve. Tears flow. Friends and loved ones offer comfort
to us. Mailboxes are stuffed full with sympathy cards, and we
receive baskets of fruit and flowers. Our homes are filled with
people to help us through. Cut off from our everyday world,
we focus on our loss.

One day, with no warning, we are informed that "it's not
the end of the world." We are expected to pick up the pieces
and to move on. Comparisons with our losses are made. "It
could have been worse," we are told. We are told that it is time
to get back to real life. We are tossed from being babied to
being bullied. In addition to our loss, we are robbed of the
dignity to mourn that loss for its own worth and in its own
time. It is as if no tragedy is enough on its own, and we could

always be worse off. Perhaps that is true to some extent, but that perspective does not make allowances for personal feelings.

Few would argue that these losses are Rites of Passage. When a son loses his father he becomes the father in his family. A couple has been together for many years and, through the process of growth, grows apart. They separate. This, too, is another Rite of Passage. The concern here is not the acknowledgement of a Rite of Passage, it is how to incorporate that viewpoint into our lives in a meaningful, dignified way.

WHEN LOVE DIES

We fall in and out of love many times in our lives. Experts on human psychology and development will tell us that this is a natural thing. Quickly they will add that our first loves, "puppy love," are nothing more than a dry run for other, more meaningful relationships. This may all be true from a certain viewpoint. Yet, how can anyone place a value on "love?" Is the intensity felt at age fifteen somehow less than that felt at thirty-two? There are worlds of differences between the two types of relationships, but can we measure that intensity? Not to the satisfaction of the person involved. Although there will be obvious differences between the endings of these relationships, there will be a period of time when those differences are moot.

Although it may seem obvious that the conclusion of a first relationship is different from a parting of the ways after many years of marriage, we tend to trivialize one and not the other. The differences lie not on the ending of one relationship and the possibility of future ones, but rather on the mechanics of picking up the pieces of the relationships and restoring personal balance.

The earth-shattering emotions that accompany "breaking up" for the first time are in many ways the worst that we experience. Here, after a time of complete trust and faith in someone of our own choosing, we are devastated to discover that we were somehow wrong in our choice. The actual reasons for the parting are not as important ultimately as is accepting the separation on its own terms. This is even more important if there are feelings of inadequacy and rejection. For a young woman, the feeling that no one will ever find her attractive again, for a young man the notion that he is clumsy and an oaf, needs to be respected before the feeling can be dismissed.

When a marriage comes to an end we must find ways to deal with both the emotional aspects of the relationship and the division of property. (Marriage in this case is being used to define a relationship where two people have lived together in a shared space for a time. There may or may not have been "legal documentation" to define the partnership.) There are many who can easily come to terms with the redefinition of the relationship but lose control when it comes to deciding who gets the favorite bookcase. Compromising and negotiating during this time will be difficult without benefit of a mediator. It is during this mediation period that much of the healing takes place, so it is advisable to look upon this as a ritual.

For every relationship that ends we are left with the hope that a new relationship will begin. This may be true, but it is the farthest thought from those who are hurt. When the ending has been reached through mutual consent, there is very little left to do. The talking that was necessary is sufficient to close those doors. Most people don't end relationships that way. The majority of us are left by someone, or leave someone. The Parting of the Ways ritual is a magickal ritual meant to be used by those who had been handfasted.

After there has been some time to adjust to the ending, the person for whom the ritual is planned should be invited to the home of a friend or family member. All those gathered should provide their favorite foods and drinks. The atmosphere should be social. With friends and family, the support network that always had been available to help the person celebrate, it is easy to have a safe space to "let go." When I experienced this kind of rejection, my Craft family gathered around and served a wonderful feast. Conversations were not staged to seduce me to speak about my loss, but everyone was aware of my mood swings regarding it. After we had eaten, I was invited to sit as a member of a circle. This was simply a circle of friends sitting together, it was not defined as a magickal space. What transpired was truly magickal.

Sitting together on the floor of a living room, the people who were most important to me spoke. Each in turn (not in order), told me something that they respected, loved or enjoyed about me. They were not flowery testimonials, just short pieces of encouragement. I was overwhelmed by their caring for me. I cried. Not anger, but releasing tears. Catharsis if you'd like. Those were healing tears that drained a good deal of the hurt. I was hugged. Daisies appeared in my arms. Laughter began. One of the men present invited me to dinner. He said that it would be a way to set the stage for many others who would ask me for dates, a form of sympathetic magick. Quickly he added that the first date is the hardest, and since we were friends we would already be comfortable together and have much to talk about. I accepted. Having been a dear friend and confidant for several years, I knew that he would never make an unwanted pass at me.

The situation was easily changed when I left my next relationship. This time my Craft family helped me to see that, since I initiated the ending, I bore the responsibility of hurting my ex-partner as little as possible. I was not responsible for growing beyond the relationship itself. Coming to understand that difference was the magick taught to me. It has helped me to close doors rather than slamming them.

PARTING OF THE WAYS

Our national divorce rate is currently around 60 percent. It would be romantic to think that a Handfasting would be some sort of preventative for divorce, but that's not the case. We make magickal mistakes too. When all avenues of reconciliation have been exhausted, a parting of the ways is necessary.

This ritual is written for a couple that will be able to continue to share a ritual space together. There will doubtless be couples who cannot perform this ritual. It is a sad commentary on our world that all too often a divorce results in so much pain and sorrow that love is replaced by hatred. When those occasions arise, it will up to the discretion of the people and family involved to find a suitable way to vary the ritual to be satisfactory both magickally and emotionally for those involved.

Prior to the ritual the couple must meet with those they have asked to perform the ritual. Here, outside of magickal space, they will discuss how property will be divided. Arrangements for child custody and visitation will be made. If there is a legal marriage as well, this can be decided in conjunction with the lawyers. With all of this done non-magickally, we clear a path for the Circle to offer a way for future healing and growth.

Invited guests should be kept to a minimum. Only those closest to the couple and the people who will be called upon for the most support should be there. If the two witnesses from the Handfasting are able to attend, their presence would be most welcome. The children of the couple should also be present for the ritual so that they are given a chance to understand that this is a parting of their parents, not an abandonment of them.

Casting the Circle

The Priestess blesses the salt and Water. She removes all negative emotions and clouded judgement from the Water, and asks for clarity and compassion. The salt is asked to lend honor and respect to the Circle. Emotional equilibrium is created by mixing the two.

Use the broom from the handfasting to sweep away resentments and confusion. This builds a place for differences to be addressed with honor.

All those gathered call the Quarters to join the Circle, then focus on the gifts that would lend healing and nurturing for the couple, rather than punishment or blame. Likewise, Goddess and God are asked to witness the parting in order to help make way for a healthier more balanced future.

Priestess: We have gathered here today to celebrate a new beginning, not to mourn an ending. _____ and _____, we are here to assist in your transitions, not to judge your decisions.

Priest: You have joined each other in celebrating many blessings of life. Together you have shared great love. Now you find that your love has grown beyond the two of you. We honor your courage to have made the decision to live separate lives.

Priestess: Once you came to this Circle to be bound because your lives were inter-woven. What has brought you here today?

The couple responds as needed.

Priest: You have exchanged tokens in the past to mark your beginning. Have you brought those tokens to be returned to mark your new beginning?

Couple gives the tokens (usually rings) to the Priestess and the Priest.

Priest: In the past we asked you both to find the meaning beyond the spoken words. Now we once again ask that you to do the same. Though there has been anger, there is no reason to withdraw respect. To do so would only belittle the love that you once shared.

Priestess: Although your paths have taken you to a crossroad where you must each go on alone, think fondly of the past and be aware that your own past has given you the strength to become the people who you are now.

Priest: You have been bound together in a magickal act. Before we can continue, is it your desire to end that bond?

The couple responds as needed.

Priestess: Then face each other now as we ask for you each to be blessed as individuals.

Priest: (*Taking incense.*) This is the gift of new beginnings. We ask that you are each blessed with the desire to find newness in the world around you.

Witness: (*Taking candle.*) This is strength and passion. We ask that each of you find the inner strength and the desire to explore new passions.

Priestess: (*Taking water.*) Here in this Water are the reflection of all your hopes and dreams. Here also are your own tears. Allow those tears to give you renewed purpose and to help you to find new dreams.

Witness: (*Taking salt.*) This salt is the symbol of your vows. Once you were bound by them, today you will be released from them. With that release comes the responsibility to not hurt one another. Draw from your experience and continue to grow.

Priestess: Now we ask the Goddess and God to lend you Their blessings as you define new paths for yourselves.

Priest: The time has come for you to return the tokens of your love to one another. Once these rings sealed your love together, now they will set your lives apart from each other with honor. Look upon them as a symbol of the cycles that always bring change.

The couple exchange rings and speak words of parting.

Witnesses: We have promised in the past to be there for you. Today we renew that promise to you, not as a couple, but as friends who have grown apart. *(They now speak personal promises to the couple.)*

Priestess: Your lives, once joined, are now separated. The binding of the past is broken as we cut your ties from each other. *(Passing a sword, athame or other cutting instrument between the couple.)* May your lives grow and be enriched in the future.

If the couple has children they are now brought to the middle of the Circle. Each parent is given an opportunity to speak to them and to ensure them of his/her love.

Priest: *(Holding the Wine and Cakes.)* We share this food together to remind us all that no matter how our lives may change, we are always nurtured by each other and by the Gods and Goddesses.

All share food and drink. Guests are now encouraged to speak to the couple (and the children) to offer their own support. When the time feels right, the people who helped to cast the Circle should close the ritual.

DEATH

The Death card appears in a Tarot reading. Fear grasps the person for whom the cards are being read. "Who is going to die?" they ask. "Death is only a transformation, offering new beginnings. It does not have to mean physical death."

An old farmer looks out over his crops. The doctors have told him that he will only live for another three months. He prepares for this year's harvest. As he cuts the grain, he knows that there will be another harvest next year and the year after.

A new mother nurses her daughter as she fights back her tears. Her mother has died that morning. Gazing into the eyes of her child she is comforted by the thought that she is now a mother for this child, and her own mother has become a daughter once again in the arms of the Mother of all life.

Of all the Rites of Passage, death is the one that challenges our spiritual, theological and philosophical beliefs the most intensely. We can shift our perspectives as many different ways as we choose, but death is final in this lifetime. Even the most devout believers in reincarnation cannot alter the fact that when a loved one passes on, *that person* is removed from our circle of friends and family. Beyond our own pain, we also need to be concerned with the feelings of others in our families (who may not share our viewpoints), so that they are also given a comfortable way in which to mourn. In some sense then, we need to find at least two different ways to incorporate our beliefs and the grieving process into our lives to effect real healing.

First we must accept the fact that many ritualize their mourning in ways that do not coincide with our ideal choices. Having been raised in a Jewish family, I still find myself confused when going to a wake. Not having a background in this ritual, I have difficulty feeling comfortable. This does not change the respect that I feel for those who see this as a vital part of the grieving process. When I sit in a church and hear the service that asks for the soul's admission to Heaven, I quietly change those words to myself and ask for the individual who has passed to have an easy transition in a way that she/he can understand. I then become actively involved in the passage.

When the deceased is someone with a shared belief system, we can take a more active role. Planning for a ritual is a major part of our own healing process. The rituals of which I speak of are not about burial or cremation, but a gathering of friends and family to say good bye to a loved one. It is within the sacred space that we will create that the tangible healing will begin. Viewing the cycles of life that touch all of us on the Earth will help to remind us that every ending offers a beginning, and all beginnings must find their own endings.

The Ritual

Friends and family sit together in a Circle. Symbols of the four elements are in the center on the altar. A bowl holding Water with hyssop oil or herb added is also on the altar. The room is lit with candles of many colors to symbolize the fullness of the world around us. If there are flowers, they should be lilies and ferns.

The Circle is drawn by everyone holding hands and repeating this phrase:

> The Circle is formed with the bonds of life
> and friendship.

Each element is picked up and passed around to all members and each one asks for the strength and blessing of the its quarter to be present. For example, in the East you might ask for new beginnings and hope, in the South for renewed strength and unbroken love, in the West for the gift of tears and memories, in the North for continuing cycles and wisdom. When all have called the elements and quarters in this way there is a moment of silence.

To invite the Gods and Goddesses into the Circle each person is encouraged to chant the name of a Goddess or a God as all intone one note. The single note will symbolize unity, the many names an expression of diversity and added strength.

Now the bowl of Water is taken by the person who was closest to the one who has passed. Gazing into the Water he/ she is given a chance to remember something significant about the loved one. If words come to her/him, she/he should feel comfortable to share a thought or memory aloud. When finished, she/he washes her/his hands in the Water and rinses her/his face with it. The bowl passed around the Circle in this manner, each person taking time to remember something or to share a thought about the person who has passed on or a friend who they are present to support.

Then it is time for those gathered to show tangible support for a friend who is mourning. Each takes up a symbol of an element or offers something, as he/she takes a moment to speak to the mourner (or mourners) about how he/she would ask for a blessing or would make a promise to him/her. The promises may vary from being available to talk in the middle of the night to cooking a meal or taking care of children. Small gifts that will help to ease some of the pain might include tapes of music, books, photos of past gatherings, or plants. What is important is that all in the Circle are allowed to express a way in which she/he can responsibly be involved in the healing process.

Tears that flow during this ritual should be welcomed quietly. Friends and family are present to share the grief, not to pass judgments. One or two of the closest family might wish to make themselves available to help dry those tears when they are needed. This often will act as a buffer so that everyday demands are not felt until everyone has had an opportunity to heal sufficiently.

After a time, food and drink should be shared, with special thanks for the continued cycle of life around us. The Circle should be closed simply, by thanking the four quarters and the Gods for Their presence. All join hands one last time and repeat this phrase as they end the ritual:

> The Circle is ended with the bonds of life and friendship. Blessed be.

MISCARRIAGE

When death takes the life of a person whom we have known and loved for years, it is difficult to not feel pain and sorrow. A miscarriage is also difficult. After an awaited pregnancy, and all of the early celebration with its anticipation, it seems cruel to lose a person before we have had a chance to meet her/him. Feelings of being cheated and denied are usually the first identifiable feelings. Later, we feel confused and punished, perhaps even guilty about something that we know we had no real control over. Thoughts of "what if" enter our minds as we search for an explanation for an inexplicable situation.

Our culture has a tendency to give the mother support and all too often ignores the father. Mothers are given a few days to rest and to recover from the physical effects, while fathers are expected to continue to go out and work. Once again we find a double standard that we should no longer tolerate. We should not accept trite words of comfort such as "it was only Nature's way to be sure that you'll have a healthy baby when the time is right." No amount of Darwinian theory will suffice either. The loss cannot be measured through comparisons.

We need to look upon this as a form of death and need to see a miscarriage as a Rite of Passage.

Ritual for the Mother

This ritual will center around a bath for cleansing. You will need a pitcher of herbal wash made up of the following:

2 parts jasmine flowers
1 part yarrow
1/2 part rue
4 drops of lotus oil
2 drops of sandalwood oil

Steep the herbs in 2 to 3 quarts of boiled Water, and allow it to cool. Strain out the herbs and add the oils.

Fill a tub with warm Water and bless it, saying:

> Mother of all life, we ask your blessings here. You who have shed tears to create the seas and rainfall, from whose Waters all life first came. It was from Your womb that we all were born and into Your cauldron that we will eventually return. Bless this Water and let our Sister and Friend feel your healing embrace. Blessed be.

The mother is assisted into the Water. All of the women present should help to bathe her with soft clothes. Speak to her about your love and concern for her. Remind her that tears will return to the Mother of All and She will help the healing process. By helping the mother to cry, you will make room for new emotions later. First the sorrow must be felt and released in order to accept the loss and to move beyond it. Here, in this Water, she can regain her own sense of power as a woman.

When the time is right, the pitcher of herbal wash is brought to the tub. It is poured over the mother as those assisting her say:

> Bless your mind, that it may once again be free to dream.
>
> Bless your eyes, that they may see the beauty and the strength that is you.
>
> Bless your heart, that it may be filled with laughter and song once again.
>
> Bless your womb, that it may heal and bring forth the gift of life when you are ready.
>
> Bless your feet, which will continue to dance the dance of the cycles.
>
> And bless your spirit, which is loved and cherished by all of us here.

Now the mother is helped out of the tub and dried off with fluffy towels. She should be nurtured with food and drink. Here, in the company of other women, she can feel safe to express her emotions and let go of the recent past in order to move into her own future.

Ritual for the Father

Some say that the mother's loss can be measured in her blood. If that is true, then the father's loss can be measured by his tears. Although there is no physical evidence of loss in the father's body, the effects of a miscarriage are as great for him as for his partner. This ritual will center on helping him to release his sorrow and to find renewed inner strength.

Ideally, this ritual is performed near running Water or near the ocean. If there is no Water nearby, then it can be adapted for the woods or a field. Even in winter, it would be best, if at all possible to go outside for the time that it takes to do the ritual. The healing properties of fresh Air and Sun are as important as the ritual acts themselves.

The father will have needed some time to prepare a petition and offering for the rite. The offering may be in the form of a small boat made from the husk and leaves of corn, or an apple cut in half. It should be something that will float if the ritual is done near Water or that will not harm the Earth if the ritual is done in the woods. The petition, a way of expressing his concern for his own family's healing, may be written on rice paper or birch bark.

All gather in a Circle and take a few moments to feel each other's presence. When the time is right, someone asks for the blessing of the God, saying:

> Seed Bearer and Great Reaper, we ask for
> Your blessings here. Your strength has given
> all seeds the ability to grow and your love has
> called each one when its time has come.
> Come to us now, as healer and teacher and
> allow our Brother to feel Your inner strength
> and find comfort. Blessed be.

The men now walk to the Water's edge or to a place in the woods. They sit with the father and speak about their feelings. Hugging and touching are important ways to convey the love that they feel and to reassure the father that he is not alone. They encourage him to speak about how he is feeling about the loss and about his partner. Tears will help to relieve some of the pain and should be welcomed. After some time, the father should take his offering and petition and leave them in the Water or in the woods. After this is done, all leave and do not look back.

Once inside again, the men place the father in the middle of Circle. The following blessing should be spoken:

> Bless your mind, that it may find peace and understand the cycles of life.
>
> Bless your eyes, that they find the blessings of the God in all things and find His reflection in you.
>
> Bless your heart, that it continue to feel love and compassion.
>
> Bless your seed, that it may give the gift of life in love and respect.
>
> Bless your feet, that will continue to dance the dance of the cycles.
>
> And bless your spirit, which is loved and cherished by all of us here.

Food and drink are shared and everyone is encouraged to share his inner feelings so that fears may be released to begin healing for the future.

ABORTION

One of the measures that our society uses to determine "adulthood" is the ability to make decisions for ourselves. The factors that must be considered for potential parenthood have never been easily defined in any culture, but in our modern world the considerations are enormous. Sometimes, a woman is pregnant and she, alone or with her partner, decides that this is not the right time to bring a new life into the world in general, or into their own family in particular. Recognizing that this decision is one of the hardest any human must face, an abortion must be looked upon as a Rite of Passage.

The ritual involves many different steps. First is the decision- making process. Getting in touch with the part of oneself that must let go of an unwanted pregnancy is stagger-ing. Those who choose to be childless must come face to face with our ever- present ability to create one. The lingering sadness can be an even greater burden for those who want a child, but for whom the time is not right.

Mediation will aid in coming to terms with the decision. This is for both of the partners if a partnership exists, or for a woman and her friends, family or spiritual teachers.

After the decision to have an abortion has been made, getting in touch with the child-spirit is the next step. Since no one is absolutely certain as to when that spirit enters the fetus, it is important for both psychological and magickal reasons to take time to express why the abortion is necessary. Once again, casting a Circle may or may not be needed; the decision is made by the people involved.

Sitting quietly, the woman should try to visualize a life's potential. Here is only energy; not a defined person, but a spirit form. Now she must gently express why this is not a good time for this spirit to come into her life. Time should be taken to outline her reasons clearly, not only for the sake of the child she cannot bear, but also to hear herself, and to accept the decision, even though it has been difficult. Sometimes the hardest decisions are the ones that empower us the most.

Next, her partner should take time to explain his part of the reason. Hearing his words will add to the self-empowering benefit of decisions made. Other members of the Circle may add their own words for the couple and for the community's healing.

After the surgery is over, there should be one final step for the couple. A ritual cleansing bath should be taken by both, either together or separately. Herbs and oils may be added to the Water as follows:

> woodruff, to heal the mind
> hyssop, to relieve sorrow
> lotus oil, for the soul and heart
> sea salt, for body and spirit.

The couple should call upon the names of Goddesses and Gods to hear the sorrow and to lend Their aid in healing and comforting. The names chosen should be those that have the most meaning for the couple involved.

They feel their sorrow leave them as they sit in the warm scented Water. If possible, family or friends should help in the bath by pouring Water over them. Returning sadness to the Mother, the couple emerges feeling relieved.

The emotional price of an abortion cannot be sidestepped, but this ritual can help the healing process begin. The presence of other family members will assure that the support needed will always be there. Ritual cannot alter the past, but it can make passage to the future less frightening.

EXPLAINING DEATH TO CHILDREN

"Mommy, Grandpa is dead. Can he really hear you?" a child asked of his mother. She had been speaking to her father as he lay inside his casket, assuring him that the family would be well and wishing him an easy transition.

"Yes. His spirit is still with us and he can hear," came the reply.

"Then where is he?"

That has to be among the hardest questions our children will ask us. Difficult not only because this is an emotionally trying time, but also because of the desire to protect our children from the harsh realities of life while trying not to distort the truth. Everything we feel in our hearts and minds must be explained with total honesty. We bare our own souls to our children as we explain, through our own grief, that the cycle of life goes on even when it moves beyond our eyes.

Most families introduce death to their children when a family member dies. I have, however, met an occasional adult who was well beyond twenty-one before someone close to him/her died. People need to understand this transition at an earlier age than that. It might be a good time to begin if a four-legged member of the family dies. Watching the news certainly provides ample opportunity to address the topic. However you decide to approach death, you need to remember that for children, death has a different impact than it does for adults. When we move from one location to another and children never see old schoolmates again, for them those schoolmates are the same as dead because for the child they are forever gone. Crushing a bug has a very different meaning for a three-year-old, who does not yet have the full capacity to understand, than it does for an eleven- or twelve-year old.

It is important for our children to grow healthy and to have a complete view of the cycle of life and death. We need to find a way to approach death that is not scary or too "airy-fairy." Sitting in a meadow is one way to begin. We see dandelions all around us, lovely yellow flowers growing freely like the Sun. Bees are collecting their pollen. There are also several puff balls from the mature dandelions. What child has not enjoyed blowing upon the seeds to watch them scatter in the wind? Ask your child where the puff balls have come from. Blow upon them. Where do the seeds go? They scatter and plant themselves and grow once again as dandelions. Sometimes they are carried by the wind for many miles before they find good soil. Others are quickly replanted and grow nearby.

"Where did Grandpa go? He is part of the wind and the Sunshine all around us. His spirit has moved on, beyond his own body. He will move to a place where he will begin again. We can still hear him singing in the leaves of the trees and he can still hear us when we speak to him."

OTHER TEARS

Tears of sorrow are not reserved only for death and ending relationships. Each of us is faced with many kinds of loss and tragedy throughout our lifetime. Many of us will receive bad news from the medical community, telling us that we have a disease that cannot be cured. AIDS and cancer are two that spring to mind immediately. Physical challenges, such as the loss of a leg or an arm no longer seem as life-threatening as they once did. Now, with modern technology, we can get around in spite of those kinds of challenges. Yet, the impact for those who must face some kind of terminal situation can be devastating.

It is not my purpose to delve into the psychological factors involved in coming to terms with this kind of grief. Nor would it be fair simply to state that these are Rites of Passage and need to be seen that way, and be done with it (although

I will admit the temptation is there). There are spiritual paths that would see these as some sort of penance for a past transgression, or as a test of faith. My personal belief system does not have a place for either of those ideas. Nor do I pretend to understand why those whom I love must suffer. Faith being what it is, I prefer to allow both God and Goddess to understand the whys and, for myself, I to learn to cope.

I have a very dear friend who has had a lifetime filled with these challenges. Her son was born with a brain dysfunction and no one knows how independent he will become. She herself has dealt with cancer. Close friends are HIV positive. Never have I heard her lament over these things. Each tear that she has shed has left her a stronger person, more resolved to find a way through.

She wrote a meditation about Death, but it can be adapted to confront Fate, to come to understand what has happened. I include it here in a modified form, because it helps to place things into a perspective that I believe makes a difference.

First, relax. Take a few breaths to clear your mind. Feel yourself becoming one with the Earth under you, and the world around you. There is no fear in this place. You are at peace. Breathe deeply and relax.

You are standing on a road. The countryside is familiar and friendly. The sky is clear above you and you can hear birds singing. You walk along this road. In the distance you can see a figure far away. You walk towards them. You are not afraid. There is no fear or pain on this road.

As you come closer to this figure you recognize Death (Fate). You are not afraid. It is not yet your time. You may safely approach. There is no pain. Death (Fate) has come to speak with you. You may ask any question except "when." Death (Fate) will respond.

You are given a chance to ask and to understand. You walk together and speak. You have no fear and you speak freely. You feel safe to cry or to shout in anger. Death (Fate) will hear you and help you. You walk together down the road.

[Spend some time considering this conversation.]

Now you have come to a crossroad. It is not your time. Death (Fate) leaves you here. You will not walk with him. You have had a chance to speak and you have been given some answers. You are not afraid, and you feel no pain. You walk down your road, alone now. Death (Fate) has walked down the other road and can no longer be seen. You walk along the beautiful country road until you return to your home. You are safe now. Your questions have been answered and you open your eyes again.

Breathe deeply and feel the world around you and the Earth beneath you. You are home again.

This meditation should be done more than once. In fact, it is suggested that this technique for self-empowering be used at least twice a year. We all grow richer in understanding by allowing ourselves, or those to whom we are close, an opportunity to confront the things that have caused the most fear. Being at peace with a situation that we cannot alter, no matter how much we would choose to, is a major part of the healing process.

There are other tears that each of us faces in life. There will be tears of disappointment and rage. We will cry when we lose jobs and when friendships end. Material things will be broken, and tears will flow. If we can recognize the fact that we can create a safe place for healing one another by interweaving spirituality and community, then our tears will eventually lead to a stronger, healthier world for us and for our children.

CONCLUSION: EVERY DAY IS A RITE OF PASSAGE

Every Circle has its own beginning and ending. All things in our world are part of even greater cycles. When you take the time to see each day as its own wonderful, magickal Circle, you move beyond the world of common people and join with those they have called "Witches." When every act becomes a magickal deed, each thought part of the greater universe, you will have crossed the boundaries between the worlds.
—from a traditional initiation ritual

Ancient myths and stories tell of how the Sun and the Moon are reborn each day, and of how these celestial bodies must move in a prescribed direction, never altering their courses. These myths give us the notion that we cannot go back and change what has passed, but must see each day as a time to begin anew. Looking beyond the literal level of these stories, they are seen as metaphors for looking at every day as a unique Rite of Passage.

While we are all born with the ability to tap into ancient knowledge, and have the capacity for great spiritual advancement, we must still live each day as a unique experience. We stop trying to "do magick" and begin to "live magickally" when we view each day as a unique opportunity to grow.

By shifting our perspective in this way, each morning brings with it a new Circle, a new beginning. It is how we greet the day, with what intent, that will determine how the entire day is likely to progress. My own experience has been that a few moments of sincere meditation each morning leaves me in a better frame of mind to get through the day. The morning meditation need not take more than a few moments. Intent is what is most important, not the total number of words spoken or thought. I begin each day (on a good day, that is) by asking both Goddess and God into my day. The following meditation may be changed to suit the specific needs of the day.

> Bless me God and Goddess, for I am Your child.
> Bless my mind, that I may think clearly and fairly, and
>   know Your wisdom.
> Bless my eyes, that I may try to see the beauty in the
>   world around me.
> Bless my heart, that I may feel the love given me and
>   not be embittered by pain.
> Bless my feet, that they may walk gently on the Earth,
>   always aware of Your presence.
> Bless my hands, that they may help me and those
>   around me.
> And bless me by Your presence this day, for I am
>   Your child.

On really bad days I will repeat this meditation in varied forms to help keep me focused on what it is that I am trying to accomplish. It also works wonders when I feel that I am about to lose my temper. I have taught it to my children in a simplified form to give them a tool with which to take more control of their lives.

While I will make no claims to being able to cure the ills of the world with this, I can safely say that it has helped me through many situations, and has kept my perception focused on growth rather than pain.

EACH MEAL IS ANOTHER
PART OF THE CYCLE

Many years ago I had a chance to study Jewish mysticism with a Hassidic Rabbi. Before we began to look at esoteric texts and to unfold the mysteries of the universe, he taught me to look upon each daily act as sacred. Before my first meal with him, he closed his eyes and began to say a blessing. I asked if he gave thanks before each meal. The reply that I received was among the most important and significant things ever taught to me. Yes, he was saying thanks for the food, but not in the manner that I was thinking of it. By his very act of acknowledging his meal, everything involved with getting that food to his plate was elevated. Each grain eaten and walked upon, by animal and person, the people involved with preparation and shipping, the cashiers, the cooks, all of these were elevated by his taking time to acknowledge the food. Even the so-called inanimate objects, such as the rocks and Water near the food source, and the sky above, the Earth below, everything was somehow blessed by this simple act. It was from that day on that I can honestly say that I have been able to look for the interconnectedness of everything around me.

Saying a thanks before eating is an excellent way of sharing our beliefs with our children. It reminds us all that before food came from the grocery store, it came from plants and animals, and was prepared by people so that we might eat. My daughter wrote a lovely mealtime grace when she was eight years old. It goes:

> Thank you God and Goddess
> for the things You gave to us;
> The fruit, the wheat,
> The milk, the meat,
> The things that we all eat.

I'm not sure that my children understand the finer points of metaphysics, but I do know that they have already begun to develop a deep connection with all of the parts of our world that work together to help each of us. We further demonstrate this by having a lit candle for at least one family meal each day. Usually our dinner is the meal where we can relax so this is when we light the candle and ask for the direct presence of the Goddess at our table, to share our meal and bless us with Her presence. A libation bowl is placed in the center of the table. We place the first pieces of the food in the bowl as an offering of thanks for the bounty with which we have been blessed. We are able to place a small portion of food aside even in McDonald's. After our meal is finished, we take the libation outdoors and leave it there. If it so happens that the birds or four-legged creatures carry it off that, too, is wonderful.

FINDING THE GODS ALL AROUND

If each act can be viewed as sacred, then why not look upon each person as the embodiment of Goddess and God? Using the maxim "As above, so below," we try to apply that idea to people and not only to magickal acts. When we meet someone by chance, and our consciousness about them looks for hidden sparks of divinity, then we see not only the wrinkles in their personalities, but also the hidden strength and beauty. Every person has a story to tell, a lesson to teach. This little shift in awareness helps to remind us that each day is a learning experience, a ritual that will lead toward more inner growth.

Children are naturals at this game. They have imaginations that have not yet been censored by a society and a culture that passes judgement on everything. We should include them in our attempts to change our perspective and grow by seeing the world through their eyes. And we need to remember our responsibility to not pass on our own shortcomings and prejudices. They will see right through any falsehoods in our attempts to be "white light" when we need to express something less than the purest ideals. Our honesty with them will keep the balance alive, and will reveal that not everything must be wonderful, that the world has its dark places. Read myths and fairy tales with them and they will become aware of these less friendly parts of the world, and will be better able to incorporate balance into their own lives.

Further challenges would be to look for signs of the Goddess in the men in our lives, and signs of the God in the women. People with whom we have had differences in the past will have changed, and we can look for signs of growth, as well. Lastly, we need to hold a mirror to ourselves. Are we able to find the reflection we have sought in others when we look into our own eyes? Without an honest recognition of our own worth, all of the work that has gone before will be insignificant. Take the time to enjoy a part of yourself each day. Soon you will find yourself seeing the reflection of the Gods in the trees around you, or the Goddess in the flock of birds overhead. Each living thing takes on a new meaning and we see far beyond our own eyes. We marvel at the grass that insists on growing out of the concrete and the shear tenacity of wildflowers along roadsides. We find beauty in the world by looking for beauty around us. This is powerful transformative magick: you might smile more than you did in the past. Be careful!

ENDING THE DAY

"Mommy, I'm ready for bed. Can I have a star?"

This is the way our family's nightly ritual begins.

Each day offers many ways for us, and our children, to grow. Our children sometimes feel this more than we do, because so much changes for them every day. We watch them struggling with the complexities of their world and try to protect them from the complexities of ours. Learning to achieve each goal is a full- time job. Sometimes it's easy to mark the beginning and the end, at other times the lines seem fuzzy. Ritual exists to help both adults and children to see the significance in the beginning, middle and end of all things.

Our family view is to see each day as a Circle, complete within itself. My children perceive this on a very instinctual level, so we have a simple ritual that closes the day for them, and us, in a way similar to the closing of a magick Circle.

Onto their foreheads I trace a pentagram, a five pointed star, with my finger, and say:

"This is a star to wish upon."

I trace a circle around it and say:

"And a Sun to brighten your path."

Now a crescent Moon on top:

"The Moon to sing to."

I kiss my finger and touch the center, and say:

"Goddess give you sweet dreams."

This is one of the first rituals that I wrote for my children. It is a special way of closing our day and saying to them "you are important to me, and to the Goddess and God." Each night they would come to me ask for their star. The few moments it takes is quickly rewarded by the smiles on their faces. The ritual was written with my own children in mind, and bedtime has always been a warm and cuddly time for our family.

One night, I was depressed as they came for those stars. Short-tempered, I told them to "go away." Their eyes flashed in surprise, and then in inspiration. Walking over to me, they gave me a star! No longer a children's ritual, we have planted the seeds for a family tradition. Now dolls and furry friends get stars at night. We have even found that a star can make scary daytime events less scary. But when drawn at night, it seems to protect us from bad dreams.

We have explored ways of looking for milestones in our lifetimes. We celebrate special experiences with rituals to highlight their significance in our lives. We bring magick into every day by looking for magick in everyday life. Every day, not just special days as noted on calendars or in appointment books.

The challenge to grow and to learn from the world around us is renewed as we begin each day. Opportunities are manifest and are taken. Our growth is measured by the ways in which we incorporate these opportunities and transform ourselves. Not every day will yield great revelations, but with a change in attitude and practice we can let go of bad days more easily and cherish the good ones even more.

Rituals need not be full dramatic affairs with months or weeks of preparation. They can occur any time you choose to shift awareness to a larger, more universal perspective. Rites of Passage are also not always dramatic events, but often are subtle changes that enrich our lives. As we grow to accept this part of our paths, we imbue everything around us with a deeper significance and a lasting beauty. Even anger and rage become powerful, positive tools for this growth, not explosive, isolated events destined to leave us lonely. All things change and grow in the world around us; celebrating those changes, we celebrate life itself.

CREATION OF RITUALS

There are many kinds of rituals that may be performed in our lifetimes. No matter what kind of ritual, there are basic guidelines for ensuring that rituals flow easily and naturally. This is a list of the elements of ritual, and how to use them in creating your own. The freedom to pick and choose from among these elements is what keeps the rituals fresh and vital. Be creative and free!

1. Creation of Sacred Space

Sweeping the area—we remove unwanted influences from the physical space of the ritual.

Mixing salt and Water—for balancing thoughts and emotions.

Casting the Circle—the drawing of physical boundaries to assist in the groups' focus.

Blessing with the elements—we take pieces of the Universe around us (Earth, Air, Fire, Water) to give life to our Circle.

Calling the Quarters—inviting the Spirits of the Directions to share Their gifts with all gathered in the Circle.

Inviting Goddess and God—calling upon the spark of All Life, we give a deeper dimension to our own Circle and to our own lives.

2. Statement of Intent. We gain focus as a group by clearly expressing why this ritual is being held.

3. Performing the Ritual. In Sacred Space we emphasis personal or group transformation by using symbols and ritual drama to celebrate a stated purpose. In short, we work magick.

4. Sharing the Experience. We underscore our community by inviting those in attendance to share their thoughts and feelings about the ritual itself. With the added dimension of the Circle's energy, stories and songs become acts of love and caring.

5. Wine and Cakes. A living symbol not only of the union that creates all life, that is also a symbolic meal to be shared by all. Nurturing each other with food symbolizes our nurturing each other's spirit, as well.

6. Closing the Circle. Saying good-bye to both Goddess and God, and the Four Directions, we ask for a conclusion. This helps to re-integrate us into our everyday world.

7. Feasting. The real magick of community continues as we share food and company with one another.

Honor and respect for all those in attendance become the constants within our Circles when rituals are based on community sharing and transformation. If the purpose of ritual is to share a part of ourselves with each other and the Gods, as we understand Them, then we need not look beyond our own hearts for inspiration. Research into myths and stories from other cultures will also enhance the natural magick and rhythm of a family working together.

APPENDIX II

TABLE OF THE ELEMENTS

AIR

Direction: East
Color: Yellow
Magickal Tool: Sword or athame
Season: Spring
Time of Life: Childhood
Time of Day: Dawn
Elemental Being: Sylphs
Some attributes: Intelligence, innocence, freedom, beginnings, psychic development, study, planning, mental processes.
Incense: (The elemental incense formulas are designed to evoke a feeling and are not based on specific planetary or magickal 2 parts woodruff

> 2 parts gum mastic
> 1 part white sandalwood
> 1 part frankincense
> 1/2 part myrrh
> 2 drops cinnamon oil
> 1 drop lavender oil

FIRE

Direction: South
Color: Red
Magickal Tool: Wand
Season: Summer
Time of Life: Adolescence

Time of Day: Noon
Elemental Being: Salamanders
Some attributes: Will, passion, creativity, movement, initiation, desire, inspiration, healing work, the hearth, purification.

Incense: 2 parts red sandalwood (santal)
1 part gum arabic
1/2 part coriander
1/4 part saltpeter
a pinch of cayenne pepper
1/2 pinch of brimstone (sulphur)
2 drops of hyssop oil
1 drop of camphor oil

WATER

Direction: West
Color: Blue
Magickal Tool: Cup or cauldron
Season: Autumn
Time of Life: Adulthood
Time of Day: Dusk
Elemental Being: Undine
Some attributes: Understanding, compassion, reflection, calm, integration, process, cleansing, nurturing, the womb, regeneration, intuition.

Incense: 2 parts gum mastic
1 part damiana
1/2 part cassia buds
1/4 part frankincense
2 drops violet oil
1 drop clove oil
1 drop cinnamon oil

EARTH

Direction: North
Color: Green
Magickal Tool: Pentacle
Season: Winter
Time of Life: Old Age
Time of Day: Midnight
Elemental Being: Gnome
Some attributes: Wisdom, surety, confidence, stability, silence, application, product, death, rebirth.
Incense: 3 parts myrrh
                    1 part patchouli
                    1 part frankincense
                    1/2 part rosebuds
                    1/2 part dittany of Crete
                    1/2 part oak moss (or 2 drops of oil)
                    1 drop civet oil

APPENDIX III

TABLE OF COLORS

Every color has its own vibratory rate. This is science. People are drawn to various colors and use them for specific purposes. This is psychology.

Our ancestors have long associated colors with specific attributes, painting the ground in colored sands, using face and body painting for ritual purposes. Our ancestors burned candles and carefully chose the color and shade of ritual robes. All was done to ensure a specific outcome. This is magick.

This is a list of the more common attributes used in modern Wicca.

White: This color is frequently associated with the
            Moon. Many people use white for the
            Goddess and God candles on the altar. White
            represents purity, protection and potential.

Yellow: The color of the East. Yellow represents new
            beginnings and childhood. It also is associ-
            ated with the Sun, and therefore represents
            higher intelligence, healing, success, friend-
            ship, happiness and enlightenment.

Red: The color of the South. Red represents
            passion, true will and expediency. The
            planetary association is Mars, lending this
            color aggressiveness and strength. Use red if

you are trying to resolve a conflict. Red also has been used by many cultures for protection from the "evil eye."

Blue: The color of the West. Blue represents serenity, reflection, meditation and healing (especially emotional). Jupiter is the ruling planet, giving the additional qualities of success (in business or financial matters), leadership abilities and honor.

Green: The color of the North. Green represents riches and richness, growth and attainment. Most often associated with Venus, green is used to represent harmony and contentment.

Pink: A color often dis-empowered in our culture, this is a good color to express love. Use pink for early childhood rituals for both girls and boys, and for Betrothals and Handfastings. Reclaim this early spring color to bring happiness and renewed strength.

Orange: The color of attraction. Orange is often used to help focus attention on the purpose of a ritual. Mercury is the associated planet, adding communication, intellect and travel.

Purple: Long known for its royal connotations, it is now used to represent justice and order. It is a good color to use for inspiration, perhaps placed in the library or working area of a home.

Lavender: Now used to represent solidarity, this color is good for uniting intention in a room. When used in ritual, it is the symbol of a meeting of the minds (Handfastings) and of spiritual growth.

Turquoise: This gentle blend of blue and green highlights many Native People's art. Drawing its own symbolism from the union of Water and Earth, reflection and growth, it represents insights.

Brown: A color associated with the Earth and grounding, brown may be used for stability and centering. It also is a good color to send back any unwanted thoughts or feelings, allowing the Earth to ground and transform them.

Black: This is the most misunderstood of all colors. Associated with darkness, it has been used as a catch-all for anything negative in nature or anything frightening. Saturn is the ruling planet, so it is a color associated with learning to overcome obstacles and limitations.

Silver: Associated with the Moon, use silver to represent the Goddess.

Gold: Associated with the Sun, gold can be used to represent the God.

APPENDIX IV

RITUAL BATHS

Many traditions include the use of a ritual bath for preparation before entering the Circle. Taking the bath helps to center attention on the ritual about to take place to release everyday thoughts, feelings and attitudes.

In order to facilitate these changes, the preparation of the bath becomes a ritual of its own. Here again, there are no hard and fast rules to be followed, but understanding why these things are done will allow the reader more room to make changes, when necessary. This bath becomes the embodiment of the Mother's womb, a place comprised of all of life's elements. So, we ask for the blessing and gifts of the four elements to fill the tub and the Water.

A tub should be filled with warm Water. Candles should be lit to illuminate the room. You will need:

> incense for the Air
> a candle for the South
> Water for the West
> sea salt for the North.

Water used for ritual purposes may be blended together from ocean, river, spring, rain and melted snow. Use at least some Water from a free-running source and one from the Mother's tears.

After filling the tub, take the incense and hold it over the Water, saying:

Spirits of Air, bless this Water. Help each
who enter to breathe away any thoughts that
would cloud their minds. Help them to
remember the song of the Sky Father and to
be filled with Your gift of freedom. Blessed
be.

Next, hold the candle over the Water, saying:

Spirits of Fire, bless this Water. Your inspiration is felt in all acts of creativity. Let all who
enter feel their own creative energies renewed.
Blessed be.

Pour a little Water into the tub, saying:

Spirits of Water, bless this bath. As you are
the tears of the sorrow and the joy of the
Mother, flowing from Her as the tides and
the rain, let all who come here feel the love of
the Mother in these Waters. Blessed be.

Place a few handfuls of salt in the bath as you say:

Spirits of Earth, bless this Water. Cleanse
away fears and stress from all who enter. Let
each person feel the warm embrace of the
Mother Earth, and know that Her wisdom is
for all to share. Blessed be.

Now all should enter the bath, either one at a time or in
couples. Sitting in the bath Water, visualize yourselves returning to the primal womb and emerge feeling renewed and
recharged.

Suggested incenses for the bath:

> Sandalwood is soft and is enhanced by the moisture in the room. Burn for relaxation and purification.
>
> Jasmine will lighten the heart and mind. This sweet incense works well for rituals of union and beginnings.
>
> Lotus has long been used for purification rituals that involve women. The oil was part of an anointing formula for new priestesses. As an incense it ties us to our past.
>
> Patchouli lends an air of mystery and seduction. Known for its properties as an aphrodisiac, use it for handfastings and betrothals.

For those who enjoy blending herbs and oils to be used atop charcoal, I suggest the following formulas:

> 1 part sandalwood
> 1 part rosewood
> 1/2 part tonka bean (powdered)

This is good for making wishes come true.

> 1 part gum mastic
> 1 part cassia buds
> 1/2 part juniper berries

Sweet and warm, I use this blend for rituals of self empowerment.

1 part frankincense
1 part myrrh
1/2 part rosebuds
1/2 part lavender
1/2 part chamomile
1/2 part vervain
1/4 part rue

A good all-purpose incense for use in both bath and ritual.

APPENDIX V

ANOINTING RITUALS

After a ritual bath, and occasionally in lieu of a bath, some people will choose to perform an anointing ritual. This is a simple ritual that focuses attention on our higher selves. We bless ourselves by placing oils on key places on our bodies and visualizing our connection to the Goddess and God.

Here is a ritual that can be used for general purposes and will provide a good framework for creating others.

Place a drop of oil on yourself while saying:

Head: Bless me God and Goddess, for I am your child.

Third Eye: Bless my mind, that I may know Your wisdom.

Throat: Bless my voice, that I may speak with love and caring.

Heart: Bless my heart, that I may feel love and strength in the world around me.

Womb: Bless my womb, the center of my creativity, as Your womb has given creative energy to all of us.

Phallus:	Bless my seed, that I may know the gift of new beginnings and growth.
Feet:	Bless my feet, which have led me to my path.
Hands:	Bless my hands, which are instruments of creation and healing.
Head:	Bless me God and Goddess, for I am Your child.

The oil used may be any scented oil that evokes a feeling compatible with the ritual. An older formula, which had no particular scent, may be used. Mix together a pure olive oil with an equal part of wine. Then add a little salt and mix thoroughly. You can use this as a base and then add a few drops of scented oil. Keep in mind that many oils in their pure form can burn or irritate the skin, so test your oils before performing a self-anointing ritual with them.

A SELECTED BIBLIOGRAPHY

Most of what I have learned about Wicca was taught to me by a family from the Welsh-English border. They were a family of great integrity and personal ethics. The things I learned were not always traceable to written text, but their love and beauty never prompted me to look beyond my own heart's belief in them.

There are many books written about modern day Wicca, this is a partial list of books that I have found helpful and interesting.

Beck, Renee and Sydney Barbara Metrick. *The Art of Ritual: A Guide to Creating and Performing Your Own Rituals for Growth and Change*. Berkeley: Celestial Arts, 1990.

Eisler, Riane. *The Chalice And The Blade: Our History, Our Future*. San Francisco: Harper and Row, 1987.

Farrar, Stewart. *What Witches Do*. 2d ed. Washington, D. C.: Phoenix Publications, 1983.

Farrar, Stewart and Janet. *Eight Sabbats For Witches*. Washington, D. C.: Phoenix Publications, 1981.
The Witches Way. Washington, D. C.: Phoenix Publications.

Gardner, Gerald B. *Witchcraft Today*. London: Rider, 1954.

Gimbutas, Marija. *The Goddesses And Gods Of Old Europe*. Berkeley: University of California Press, 1982.

Graves, Robert. *The White Goddess*. 3d ed. London: Faber and Faber, 1952.

LeLand, Charles G. *Aradia, Gospel of the Witches*. London:

C.W. Daniel Co., 1984.

Murray, Margaret A. *The Witch Cult In Western Europe.* London: Oxford University Press, 1921.

Rees, Alwyn and Brinley. *Celtic Heritage.* London: Thames and Hudson, 1961.

Ryall, Rhiannon. *West Country Wicca.* Washington: Phoenix Publications, 1990.

Spence, Lewis. *Mysteries of Britain.* Scot Press, 1988.

Starhawk. *The Spiral Dance.* San Francisco: Harper and Row, 1979.

ABOUT THE AUTHOR

Tzipora Klein currently tours the country with her husband, Kenny, playing folk music and telling stories. They have shared many adventures and wonders with their children, Maeghan and Jesse.

Tzipora was born in Brooklyn, New York, and was raised in a Reform Jewish family. She began studying the Craft in the early 1970s. Near the beginning of 1977, Tzipora co-founded Blue Star, a tradition-based neo-Pagan system that has formed a network that reaches across the United States and into Canada. Blue Star strives to attain Tzipora's goal of living magically by incorporating traditional values of the Craft into the modern world.